William Cowper, William Trego Webb

Shorter Poems

William Cowper, William Trego Webb

Shorter Poems

ISBN/EAN: 9783744710855

Printed in Europe, USA, Canada, Australia, Japan

Cover: Foto ©Thomas Meinert / pixelio.de

More available books at **www.hansebooks.com**

COWPER'S SHORTER POEMS.

COWPER'S
SHORTER POEMS

EDITED
WITH INTRODUCTION AND NOTES

BY

W. T. WEBB, M.A.
LATE PROFESSOR OF ENGLISH LITERATURE, PRESIDENCY COLLEGE, CALCUTTA;
EDITOR OF "COWPER, THE TASK, BOOK IV.," "SELECTIONS
FROM COWPER'S LETTERS," ETC.

𝔏𝔬𝔫𝔡𝔬𝔫
MACMILLAN AND CO., LTD.
NEW YORK: MACMILLAN AND CO.
1896

GLASGOW: PRINTED AT THE UNIVERSITY PRESS
BY ROBERT MACLEHOSE AND CO.

PREFACE.

IT is hoped that this volume, while not exceeding the limits suitable to a book for the class-room, includes all the best of Cowper's shorter poems. In the Introductions prefixed to the Notes, and in the Notes themselves, I have not scrupled to quote freely from his Letters, both for their interest as commentaries upon the poems, and for their value as an index to the poet's feelings and character. For, as Sainte Beuve remarks, " You apprehend the true sources of his poetry, of the true poetry of the home and of private life, best in his letters : the affectionate rallying, the familiarity which despises nothing of any interest as too humble and too little, side by side with loftiness, or rather with depth."

The poems are arranged in the order of their first publication. In the case of three of them—*The Poplar Field, Gratitude,* and *To Mrs Unwin*—I have, I think, shown in my preliminary Introductions that the generally received date of their composition is of very doubtful authenticity.

In the preparation of this book I have consulted the Globe Edition of Cowper's Poetical Works, edited

by the Rev. Canon Benham, and the Aldine Edition,
edited by Mr. Bruce. For much, too, that is valuable
in my General Introduction and Notes, my grateful
acknowledgments are due to the Rev. H. T. Griffith's
edition of Cowper's Poems in the Clarendon Press
Series, and to the excellent *Life of William Cowper* by
Mr. Thomas Wright, Principal of Cowper School,
Olney. I have also to express my indebtedness for a
few illustrations contained in my Notes to Professor
J. W. Hales's *Longer English Poems*, and to Mr. C. H.
Tawney's annotations on four of Cowper's poems.

W. T. W.

CONTENTS.

vii

GENERAL INTRODUCTION.

WILLIAM COWPER was born on the 15th of November (Old Style), 1731, at Great Berkhampstead, in Hertford-shire—a parish of which his father was rector. His mother was a Donne, of the same family as the poet of that name, and descended by several lines from Henry III. She died when Cowper was six years old, and he was sent to a boarding-school. In 1741 he was entered at Westminster School, of which Dr Nichol was Headmaster, with Vincent Bourne as one of the under-masters, and which he left at eighteen. He was soon after articled to an attorney in London, in whose office Thurlow, the future Lord Chancellor, was his fellow-clerk. In 1752 he took chambers in the Temple, and in 1754 was called to the Bar. In the former year he was seized with his *first derangement*. During these years much of his time was spent at the house of his uncle, Ashley Cowper, with his daughters, Harriet (afterwards Lady Hesketh) and Theodora Jane, with whom he fell in love, and who is the "Delia" of his early love-poems. His uncle, however, refused to sanction his daughter's engagement, and the lovers were finally parted. She is no doubt the "Anonymous" of his *Letters*, who gave him many substantial proofs of her unaltered affection. He gave his time to literature and the society of the wits of the "Nonsense Club" rather than to law, and renewed his connexion with his old school-fellows, Churchill, Colman, Lloyd, and Thornton. Another old school-fellow was Joseph Hill, who ever after remained his staunch and helpful friend. In 1763 he received the nomination to the office of Clerk of the Journals of the House of Lords, but visions of opposition to the appointment, and fears of his own incapacity so wrought upon a mind already weakened by an attack of melancholy arising from his lonely surroundings, that he went mad (his *second derangement*) and attempted suicide, his madness taking the form of religious despair. After eighteen months in Dr. Cotton's private asylum at St. Albans he recovered, and in 1765 was placed by his relatives at Huntingdon. Here he met the Unwin family, with whom he lived for the next two years. On the death of Mr. Unwin senior, he accompanied his faithful friend and companion, Mrs. Unwin (the "Mary" of his *Letters* and poetry), to "Orchard Side," a house close to the vicarage at Olney, in Buckinghamshire, on the river Ouse, where he came under the influence of the Rev. John Newton, curate of the town. In 1773 his old malady again overtook him (his *third derangement*), and he again attempted self-destruction. After his recovery he diverted his mind with gardening—a favourite pursuit—with carpentering, and with drawing; and found amusement in keeping three tame hares. In 1780 a period of literary activity began, and at Mrs. Unwin's suggestion he produced his First Volume, comprising *The Progress of Error*, with the other Moral Satires, which was published in March, 1782. Meanwhile, in 1781, Cowper formed the acquaintance of Lady Austen, who subsequently came to live at Olney, and who inspired the *Task* as well as *John Gilpin*. These two poems, with *Tirocinium* and the *Epistle to Joseph Hill*, made up his Second Volume, which was published in July, 1785. Early in 1782 a temporary estrangement occurred between Lady Austen and the poet, but before the publication of the *Task* a lasting rupture took place, and in May, 1784, she finally left Olney. At this time he became intimate with the Throckmortons, and in the same year he began his translation of Homer, which was finished in September, 1790, and published in July, 1791. In June, 1786, Lady Hesketh paid him a visit, and by her care and liberality he and Mrs. Unwin were transferred to "Weston Lodge," a house belonging to Mr. Throckmorton at Weston Underwood, a village about a mile from Olney—a removal which was closely followed by the death of William Unwin. In the following year occurred his *fourth derangement*, and in December, 1791, Mrs. Unwin's health began to fail. He now undertook an edition of Milton, which brought him into communication with Hayley, to whom in August, 1792, he paid a visit of six weeks at Eartham, near Chichester. In January, 1794, came the final breakdown, which necessitated the removal of himself and the now helpless Mrs. Unwin to Mundesley, on the Norfolk coast. In October, 1796, they were taken to East Dereham, in Norfolk, where soon after Mrs. Unwin died. Mentally shattered,

Cowper survived her three years and a half, and died
very peacefully on April 25th, 1800, and was buried
in Dereham Church.

His Times.   Cowper lived in stirring times, the events of which
he viewed with interest "through the loopholes of
retreat" by means of that "map of busy life," the
The Young   newspaper. When he was fourteen years of age occurred
Pretender.
the invasion of the Young Pretender, in 1745 his
victory over Sir John Cope at Prestonpans, and his
final defeat at Culloden in 1746.

Wars with   During the first fifty years of Cowper's life England
France, Spain,
and America. was almost continually at war with France or Spain
or both together. The War of the Austrian Succes-
sion led to hostilities with France in 1744, and in
1759 the capture of Quebec by Wolfe made Canada
a British possession. In 1762, in consequence of the
Family Compact, war was declared against Spain, which
was followed by the Peace of Paris in 1763. In 1775
the American War began—the result of an attempt to
impose import duties on the British Colonies in North
America. The battles of Lexington and Bunker's Hill
in 1775. were followed by the American Declaration
of Independence in 1776, and in the following year,
under the Convention of Saratoga, General Burgoyne
surrendered to the American General Gates. This
was the turning-point of the war, and France in
1778 and Spain in 1779 entered into an alliance
with the American States ; while in 1780 England,
in self-defence, declared war against Holland—a year
that was marked by Rodney's famous victory over
the Spanish fleet off Cape St. Vincent. The same

year saw all the powers of Europe arrayed against
Britain under the "Armed Neutrality" compact,
which claimed that a neutral flag should protect all
cargoes. From 1779 to 1782 Gibraltar, bravely de-
fended by Elliot, was besieged in vain by the French
and the Spanish. In 1781 Cornwallis's capitulation at
York Town resulted in the acknowledgment of the
independence of the United States in 1782; and in
1783 the Peace of Versailles was concluded with
France and Spain.

In Cowper's life-time, too, occurred the commence- Indian affairs
ment and consolidation of our Indian Empire. In
1751 Clive captured Arcot from the French, and in
1757 won the battle of Plassy. In 1765 by the
Treaty of Allahabad the revenues of Bengal, Behar,
and Orissa were ceded to the East India Company.
Warren Hastings became Governor of Bengal in 1772,
and in 1774 Governor-General of British India. In
1779 Sir Eyre Coote defeated Haidar Ali and his
Mahratta hordes at Porto Novo, and again at Polli-
lore. The younger Pitt's East India Bill, erecting a
Board of Control over the Company's administration,
was passed in 1784; and in 1785 Hastings returned
to England, was impeached in 1788 before the House
of Lords, and at length acquitted in 1795.

Another stirring event of Cowper's day was the The Gordon
"No-Popery Riots." In 1778 a Bill was passed to   Riots.
relieve the Roman Catholics of the worst of their
civil disabilities. Popular riots followed in Scotland,
and in 1780 Lord George Gordon convened a monster
meeting of Protestants in St. George's Fields, who
marched to the House of Commons and burst into

the lobby. For five days (June 2–7), owing to the want of energy shown by the authorities, London was at the mercy of the mob, who burned down not fewer than 72 private houses, with four or five strong gaols. Gordon was tried on a charge of high treason, and acquitted in 1781.

French
Revolution.

In 1789 the first French Revolution commenced with the meeting of the National Assembly on June 17, and the storming of the Bastille on July 14. In 1790 a new Constitution was forced upon the king, who in 1791 attempted to escape from France, but was stopped at Varennes and brought back to Paris. In 1792 the ill success of the French arms against the Continental powers caused a fresh outburst of revolutionary excitement at Paris, and on August 10th the Tuilleries was stormed by the mob, an event which was followed by a terrible massacre, lasting five days (Sept. 2–7), of imprisoned royalists. On September 21st, France was declared a Republic, and in January, 1793, Louis XVI. was executed. The Reign of Terror followed in the same year, and the execution of the queen, Marie Antoinette. In 1795 the Government of the Directory was established, accompanied by the rise to power of Napoleon I.

England in
Cowper's
youth.

Of the social and political life of England in Cowper's day—or rather that of which he had experience as a young man—a modern writer has given a gloomy picture. It was a world from which the spirit of poetry seemed to have fled. Spiritual religion was almost extinct. The Church was little better than a political force. The clergy were idle and neglectful of their duties, often sordid and corrupt, fanatics in their Toryism, and cold, rationalistic, and almost heathen in their preachings. The society of the day was one of hard and heartless polish and fashionable immorality, devoted to a giddy round of theatre-going, card-parties, and balls. Among the common people religion was almost extinct. Ignorance and brutality reigned in the cottage. Drunkenness and profanity reigned in palace and cottage alike. In a letter of 1785 to Newton, Cowper writes : "Heathenish parents can only bring up heathenish children ; an assertion nowhere oftener or more clearly illustrated than at Olney, where children, seven years of age, infest the streets every evening with curses and with songs to which it would be unseemly to give their proper epithet." Gambling, cock-fighting, and bull-baiting were the amusements of the people. Political life was corrupt from the top of the scale to the bottom. Society was intensely aristocratic ; no duties towards the lower classes were acknowledged ; and each rank was divided from that below it by a sharp line, which precluded brother-hood or sympathy. Of humanity there was as little as there was of religion. It was the age of the criminal law which hanged men for petty thefts, of life-long imprisonment for debt, of the unreformed prison system, and of the press-gang. That the slave-trade was iniquitous hardly any one suspected.[1]

But a change was at hand, and two revivals—one literary, and the other religious—were in progress, in both of which Cowper took no inconsiderable part. It is to him chiefly, along with Thomson, Gray, and Crabbe,

Revival of Poetry.

[1] See Goldwin Smith's *Cowper*, "English Men of Letters " Series ; and compare Cowper's own sketch in *Tirocinium*, 813-858.

that we owe that great revolution in popular taste and sentiment which substituted the "romantic" for the "classical" type in our poetic literature—a revolution which was ushered in by the publication in 1765 of Bishop Percy's *Reliques of Ancient English Poetry*. In Cowper's writings a simple and natural, almost colloquial, style takes the place of that pompous and artificial style which Pope had brought into favour; and he is one of the leaders in the reaction from the hard conventionalism and cold, unreal sentiment of the Queen Anne school of poetry, to the picturesque freshness and genuine human feeling which was to attain a yet nobler development in the hands of a Scott, a Shelley, and a Wordsworth.

With the religious revival of 1738, of which Whitfield and Wesley were the leaders, Cowper was even more in sympathy. It expressed a revolt from the religious deadness of the time, and its aim was to carry religion and morality to the masses of the population. But it did more than this; its action upon the Church broke the lethargy of the clergy, till the fox-hunting parson and the absentee rector became at last impossible. A fresh moral enthusiasm arose in the nation at large, the profligacy of the upper classes gradually disappeared, and a new philanthropic impulse established Sunday schools, raised hospitals, sent John Howard on his visits to the prisons of England and Europe, supported Burke in his plea for the Hindoo, and Clarkson and Wilberforce in their crusade against the iniquity of the slave trade.[1] Of this moral and religious movement Cowper was the poetical exponent; and his indignant

---

[1] See *Green's History of the English People*, vol. iv., pp. 273-4.

denunciations of national offences against piety and morality, with the intense religious feeling that animates his writings, mark him out from among the poets of his day, and indeed from among all other English poets.

Cowper was of an amiable and cheerful disposition, and his natural gaiety of temperament often shows itself in his poetry, and especially in his *Letters*. The pessimism with which he has been charged seems to have been the outcome partly of the hypochondria from which he constantly suffered,[1] and partly of his Calvinist theology, which inculcated "assurance of salvation," a doctrine which, in his morbid broodings over his own condition, was converted in his case into assurance of perdition.

At the same time, Cowper is never unctuous, and though he sometimes indulges in a censorious tone of thought and expression, no trace of religious cant is to be found in his writings; the refined and delicate taste that is one of his most striking characteristics, governs, with hardly an exception, his frequent references to spiritual matters. Here and there, it is true, he betrays a fanatical antipathy to natural science,[2] and the Misagathus episode in the sixth book of the *Task*[3]

Cowper's CHARACTER: (a) His natural cheerfulness.

(b) His refinement of taste.

---

[1] Cf. *Letters, To Lady Hesketh*, Nov. 23, 1785: "I have, indeed, a most troublesome stomach, and which does not improve as I grow older"; and *To Newton*, Dec. 3, 1785: "Having been for some years troubled with an inconvenient stomach; and, lately, with a stomach that will digest nothing without help."

[2] As in *Task*, iii. 150-190; cf. note, p. 104, l. 80.

[3] Ll. 483-559.

savours somewhat of a religious intolerance which is characteristic of his creed rather than of his natural character.

(c) His melan-
choly.

But if his constitutional melancholy was partially the cause of his gloomy views of life, it was this same melancholy that drove him to poetical composition, and which, at the same time, gives it a certain austerity of tone. "Dejection of spirits," he writes, "which I suppose may have prevented many a man from becoming an author, made me one. Manual occupations do not engage the mind sufficiently, as I know by experience, having tried many. But composition, especially of verse, absorbs it wholly."[1] And again: "Amusements are necessary in a retirement like mine, especially in such a state of mind as I labour under. The necessity of amusement makes me sometimes write verses; it made me a carpenter, a bird-cage maker, a gardener; and has lately taught me to draw."[2]

(d) His shy-
ness.

Another characteristic of Cowper was his excessive shyness and sensitiveness, which has been already illustrated by his morbid shrinking from the Parliamentary clerkship, and which led to a passionate love of retirement and seclusion. He calls himself " naturally the shyest of mankind," and describes how at Olney he " lived the life of a solitary," unvisited by a single neighbour.[3] The visit of a stranger generally disconcerted him, and when he is told that a "lady of quality" awaits him in the parlour, " he feels his

---

[1] *Letters, To Lady Hesketh,* Oct. 12, 1785.

[2] *Ib., To Unwin,* April 6, 1780. See also *To Lady Hesketh,* Dec. 15, 1785; and cf. *Task,* iv. 261-264.

[3] *Ib., To Hurdis,* Aug. 9, 1791.

spirits sink ten degrees." And he concludes his account of the occurrence with, "I am a shy animal, and want much kindness to make me easy. Such I shall be to my dying day."[1]

A natural concomitant of this shyness was a sympathetic tenderness of disposition, which was a perpetual protest against the hardness of the world around him, and which showed itself in his love for animals. Besides his hares, his spaniel, his goldfinches, and his cat, all of which his poetry has enshrined,[2] at one time we find "eight pair of tame pigeons" waiting for their breakfast every morning from his hand;[3] and, at another, a pet linnet is let out of its cage, "to whisk about the room a little" and then be shut up again,[4] while the gambols of a kitten are an innocent delight to him.[5] He kept, too, a tame mouse while he was a schoolboy at Westminster.[6] It is noticeable that of the thirty-seven poems contained in this volume no fewer than sixteen relate to animals. Very characteristic is a passage in one of his letters: "All the notice that we lords of creation vouchsafe to bestow on the creatures, is generally to abuse them; it is well therefore that here and there a man should be found a little womanish, or perhaps a little childish in this matter, who will make amends, by kissing, by coaxing,

(c) His tenderness of disposition.

(1) Towards animals.

[1] *Letters, To Bagot,* Aug. 2, 1791.
[2] See *Epitaph on a Hare, The Dog and the Water-Lily, The Faithful Bird, The Retired Cat,* and *The Colubriad.*
[3] *Letters, To Unwin,* Sept. 21, 1799.
[4] *Ib., To Unwin,* Feb. 27, 1780.
[5] *The Retired Cat,* Introduction.
[6] *Letters, To Lady Hesketh,* Jun. 16, 1786.

and laying them in one's bosom."[1] He tells Lady Hesketh (Nov. 23, 1785), that he has but one quarrel with King George III., viz., that he is fond of stag-hunting. Some of his most exquisite lines are those in which he describes the innocent happiness of beast or bird that people his silvan haunts;[2] the squirrel, the woodpecker, the sheep are his intimates, with whom he shares his rural retreat,[3] and the verses in which he inculcates kindness to animals have become classical on that theme.[4] He cannot dismiss the subject of the waggoner plodding beside his load in winter, without a plea for the "poor beasts" that drag it— "Ah, treat them kindly!"[5] and when he is sinking into the depths of hypochondria, he closes a touching letter with an inquiry after his "poor birds."[6]

(2) Towards the poor.

This gentle sensibility showed itself too in his friendly attitude towards the poor, and his sympathetic descriptions of their hardships and sorrows. His *Letters* contain not a few compassionate references to the sufferings of the poverty-stricken lace-makers of Olney, and what a realistic and touching picture has he drawn in the *Task*[7] of the poor cottager's winter evening— each sad detail accurately worked in with unadorned directness. There is a world of simple pathos in the single line I have italicised—

> "The taper soon extinguished, which I saw
> *Dangled along at the cold finger's end*
> Just when the day declined."

---

[1] *Letters, To Hurdis*, June 13, 1791.   [2] *Task*, vi. 305 *et seq.*
[3] See *On a Mischievous Bull* and *The Needless Alarm.*
[4] *Task*, vi. 560 *et seq.*
[5] *Ib.* iv. 370 *et seq.* ; see also ll. 147, 148.
[6] *Letters, To Buchanan*, Sept. 5, 1795.   [7] iv. 374-398.

Lastly, Cowper was pre-eminently a lover of Nature. *(f)* His love of
Slighted as it was in his day, "the country," he writes, Nature.
"wins me still";[1] and the only poets that could
please him in his youth were those

> "whose lyre was tuned
> To Nature's praises."[2]

"Everything," he writes, "I see in the fields is to me
an object, and I can look at the same rivulet, or at a
handsome tree, every day of my life with a new
pleasure. This indeed is partly the effect of a natural
taste for rural beauty, and partly the effect of habit;
for I never in all my life have let slip the opportunity
of breathing fresh air, and of conversing with nature,
when I could fairly catch it."[3] The tender care with
which he has studied her varied effects is sufficient
proof of the love he felt for her, illustrated as it is so
frequently and exquisitely in his verse. Take for
instance his description of the play of light and shade
under the "graceful arch" of an avenue of trees:—

> "Beneath
> The chequered earth seems restless as a flood
> Brushed by the wind. So sportive is the light
> Shot through the boughs, it dances as they dance,
> Shadow and sunshine intermingling quick,
> And darkening and enlightening, as the leaves
> Play wanton, every moment, every spot."[4]

Or, if we pass to his enumeration of the plants in a
greenhouse, how picturesquely accurate are the epithets

---

[1] *Task*, iv. 694 ; see note to my edition.   [2] *Ib.* 704, 705.
[3] *Letters*, *To Unwin*, Nov. 10, 1788.   [4] *Task*, i. 343-349.

he employs, and with what loving delight does he
linger over the picture :—

> " The spiry myrtle with unwithering leaf
>   Shines there, and flourishes. The golden boast
>   Of Portugal and Western India there,
>   The ruddier orange and the paler lime,
>   Peep through their polished foliage at the storm,
>   And seem to smile at what they need not fear.
>   The amomum there with intermingling flowers
>   And cherries hangs her twigs. Geranium boasts
>   Her crimson honours ; and the spangled beau,
>   Ficoides, glitters bright the winter long." [1]

In his shorter poems too we notice the same watch-
fulness of nature and her ways. The devastated poplar
field brings back to his ear the " whispering sound "
of the winds as they sang in the leaves of the trees
while yet unfelled, and reminds him how the Ouse
once gave back their image.[2] He has an eye for the
bee that vainly buzzes against the glass of his pineapple frames, and gathers a moral from the sight.[3]
The Needless Alarm is full of these natural touches.
How true to nature is his description of the grazing
flock—

> "Some with soft bosom pressed
> The herb as soft, while nibbling strayed the rest,"

till, roused by the huntsman's horn and the cry of the
hounds,

> " The sheep recumbent and the sheep that grazed,
>   All huddling into phalanx, stood and gazed,
>   Admiring, terrified, the novel strain,
>   Then coursed the field around, and coursed it round again."

---

[1] *Task*, iii. 570-579.   [2] *The Poplar Field*, 3-5.
[3] *The Pineapple and the Bee.*

We feel, as we read, that the poet had observed the whole scene for himself, and with quiet eye harvested every detail.

As has been said of Tennyson, so it is true of Cowper, that the Nature he loved was of the well-ordered and well-regulated kind, rather than the Nature of mountains and rocks and shaggy forests. He delights in the trim avenue, the carefully-tended garden, the sheltered walk, the Wilderness with its "well-rolled" paths. Writing of his visit to Hayley at Eartham, near Chichester, he says: "The cultivated appearance of Weston suits my frame of mind far better than wild hills that aspire to be mountains, covered with vast unfrequented woods, and here and there affording a peep between their summits at the distant ocean. Within doors all was hospitality and kindness, but the scenery *would* have its effect; and though delightful in the extreme to those who had spirits to bear it, was too gloomy for me."[1]

(1) He prefers well-ordered Nature.

Though Cowper, like Wordsworth, was a reverent student of Nature's lore, he never thought, like him, of idealizing her as a power that may enable us to "see into the life of things," and of listening for her hidden voices. He depicts her outward features with loving fidelity, but sees no soul behind them. The only spiritual significance Nature has for him is that she affords a proof of the wisdom and goodness of the Creator. At the same time he approaches nearer to Wordsworth's idealism than such a writer as Thomson

(2) His view of Nature differs from Wordsworth's.

---

[1] *Letters, To Newton*, Oct. 18, 1792. See also *Ib., To Lady Hesketh*, Sept. 9, 1792.

did, who merely reproduces her picturesque effects. He can contemplate her as a whole, and in one passage at least in his poetry we find a flash of still profounder imaginative insight. For the solitary man, he tells us, not only animals but shrubs and trees have speech, easy to be understood; and then follows this couplet :—

> " After long drought, when rains abundant fall,
>   *He hears the herbs and flowers rejoicing all*," [1]

the latter line of which almost startlingly reminds us of the great poet of Nature.

COWPER'S
SHORTER
POEMS :
(a) They were
suggested by
incidents.

Cowper's genius, as St. Beuve has remarked, is one that needs to be aroused; he must have someone or something to suggest to him his subjects. His First Volume was written at Mrs. Unwin's instance, and it is to Lady Austen that we are indebted for *The Task* and *John Gilpin*. It is the same with his shorter poems. A few, like *Boadicea, Alexander Selkirk*, and *Heroism*, were suggested by his reading and reflection; and a few others, like the *Epistle to Joseph Hill, The Valediction*, and the two poems addressed to Mrs. Unwin, are the natural outcome of his personal relations with others; but the large majority are prompted by little incidents of his daily life. And since the poet's *Letters* are to a large extent a chronicle of common, everyday doings and events, it is natural that we should often find there the prose original of what he afterwards turned into poetry. [2] He can

---

[1] *The Needless Alarm*, 59, 60.

[2] See Introductions to *The Poplar Field, Mrs. Throckmorton's Bullfinch, The Faithful Bird, The Dog and the Water-Lily*, and *The Colubriad*.

utilise in this manner any occurrence, however trivial.
He inadvertently snaps off the head of a rose heavy
with rain-drops, and *The Rose* is the result. A cat is
accidentally shut up in a drawer, and we get that
delightfully humorous piece, *The Retired Cat.* A viper
is found in his garden; puss and her kittens inspect
him, and Cowper kills him; there is nothing else to
tell; but out of this nothing comes the inimitable
Colubriad. The summer is hot, and the sun dries up
his ink-glass. What can be more commonplace or
unimportant? Yet out of such slight material are
evolved the seven stanzas of the admirable *Ode to
Apollo.*

That it was good for the poet to have his intellect
roused and occupied in this way Cowper himself (as
has been already pointed out) is the first to acknow-
ledge. " I am glad," he writes in a letter[1] describing
one of them, "of such incidents; for at a pinch, and
when I need entertainment, the versification of them
serves to divert me." In another letter [2] he says : " At
this season of the year, and in this gloomy uncom-
fortable climate, it is no easy matter for the owner of
a mind like mine, to divert it from sad subjects, and
fix it upon such as may administer to its amusement.
Poetry, above all things, is useful to me in this respect.
While I am held in pursuit of pretty images, or a
pretty way of expressing them, I forget everything
that is irksome, and like a boy that plays truant,
determine to avail myself of the present opportunity

(b) Their com-
position
diverted
him.

---

[1] *Letters, To Unwin,* Aug. 4, 1783.
[2] *Ib., To Newton,* Dec. 21, 1780.

to be amused, and to put by the disagreeable recollection that I must, after all, go home and be whipt again." And again: "Despair made amusement necessary, and I found poetry the most agreeable amusement. Had I not endeavoured to perform my best, it would not have amused me at all. The mere blotting of so much paper would have been but indifferent sport." [1]

(c) They were polished and revised.

This last remark reminds us of the special care that he bestowed upon these amusements of his leisure. However slight the poems might be, and however trivial their subjects, he was not satisfied till he had brought them, as far as he was able, to perfection. "With all this indifference to fame," he writes,[2] "I have taken the utmost pains to deserve it. . . . I consider that the taste of the day is refined, and delicate to excess, and that to disgust the delicacy of taste by a slovenly inattention to it, would be to forfeit at once all hope of being useful; and for this reason, though I have written more verse this last year than perhaps any man in England, I have finished, and polished, and touched, and retouched with the utmost care. If after all it should be converted into waste paper, it may be my misfortune, but it will not be my fault." This was written in reference to the approaching publication of his First Volume; but several months before he had such a prospect in view, we find him saying the same thing: "To touch and retouch is, though some writers boast of negligence, and others would be ashamed to show their foul copies, the secret of almost all good writing, especially in verse. I am never

[1] *Letters, To Newton,* Aug. 6, 1785.
[2] *Ib., To Unwin,* Oct. 6, 1781.

weary of it myself." [1]   In the letter to Unwin, enclosing his verses *On a Goldfinch*, he compares himself to a
lapidary "rubbing away the roughness of a stone,"
and pleased "if after all the polishing he can give it,
it discovers some little lustre." [2] Instances of this care are
to be found in *John Gilpin*, which we know from his
Letters underwent considerable revision ; in *Mrs. Throckmorton's Bullfinch, The Faithful Bird, The Dog and the Water-
Lily*, and *On the Receipt of my Mother's Picture* ; and in
Gratitude,[3] which was to a large extent rewritten.

With all this care and fastidiousness of taste, there *(d)* Their
is nothing laboured in Cowper's productions. He wrote facility.
with undoubted ease and grace, and threw off these
slighter pieces with a freedom and animation that
show how much he enjoyed the task. The first
draft of *John Gilpin* was composed during the wakeful
hours of a single night ; *A Fable, The Rose*, and the
Epistle to Hill were all written in one day, and the
two latter at a time when the *Task* and other engage-
ments left him but scanty intervals of leisure. A few
moments snatched from his Homeric labours gave us
The Dog and the Water-Lily. "A thought," he writes,[4]
"sometimes strikes me before I rise; if it runs readily
into verse, and I can finish it before breakfast, it is
well ; otherwise it dies, and is forgotten ; for all subsequent hours are devoted to Homer." And in the
same letter comparing himself, burdened with his task
of translation, to an ass harnessed to a sand-cart, and

[1] *Letters, To Unwin*, July 2, 1780.
[2] See Introduction to the poem.
[3] See the notes to these five poems.
[4] *Letters, To Lady Hesketh*, Jan. 19, 1788.

no longer "throwing up his heels behind, frolicksome and airy, as asses less engaged are wont to do," he says : "So I . . . seldom allow myself those pretty little vagaries, in which I should otherwise delight, and of which, if I should live long enough, I intend hereafter to enjoy my fill."

(e) They show his love of retirement and country life.

Like the *Task*, Cowper's shorter poems, as a whole, betoken the completely domesticated man, one who loves retirement and country life. Cowper is supremely contented "in the low vale of life," delighting in the thought that he is at "a safe distance" from the "great Babel"[1] of the outer world. "I am," he writes to Thomas Park,[2] "as you say, a hermit, and probably an irreclaimable one, having a horror of London that I cannot express, nor indeed very easily account for." Hence the heartfelt enjoyment with which he dwells upon the pleasures of the country and the home fireside, as opposed to the "fandango, ball, and rout"[3] of town life. What an open-air freshness there is about *The Needless Alarm* and *The Dog and the Water-Lily*, and what an abiding delight in natural objects pervades *The Poplar Field* and *The Rose !*

(f) Their humour, irony, and pathos.

Cowper's love of humour and quiet irony, so conspicuous in his Letters, is also a marked characteristic of these poems. In *John Gilpin* he lets himself go, as it were, and the verses seem an echo of the peals of laughter that were heard issuing from his bedroom on the night of its composition. But his prevailing

---

[1] *Task*, iv. 799, 93, 90.　　[2] May 17, 1793.
[3] *The Faithful Bird*, 33.

humour is of a more delicate kind, such as that which makes *The Needless Alarm* such delightful reading, and which charms us in *The Retired Cat* and *The Colubriad*. It is a humour that has an underlying vein of gentle mockery in its composition—that playful irony of which he is so consummate a master. He is careful too that these short pieces should have neatness and point; there is no wordiness, nothing slovenly about them. "Whatever is short," he writes,[1] "should be nervous, masculine, and compact. Little men are so; and little poems should be so; because where the work is short the author has no right to the plea of weariness; and laziness is never admitted as an available excuse in anything." Of this pointed compactness the *Report of an Adjudged Case* forms an excellent instance. The touches of satire to be found in Cowper's minor poems are always genial, with perhaps the one exception of *The Valediction*, in penning which we may forgive the poet if he considered that he did well to be angry. Along with its humour, his poetry possesses in no small degree the closely allied quality of pathos; and it may well be doubted whether there are two short poems by any author in any language that are instinct with such a tender and delicate, and yet deep and heartfelt emotion as the lines *On My Mother's Picture* and *To Mary*. In *The Castaway* Cowper rises to an even higher level. As an expression of the pathos of utter despair it is marked by a sublimity very rarely attained by the poet elsewhere.

Cowper fully recognised the function of the poet to *(g)* Their "morals."

---

[1] *Letters, To Unwin*, July 2, 1780.

be the teacher of mankind. " My principal purpose," he writes of the *Task*, " is to allure the reader, by character, by scenery, by imagery, and such poetical embellishments, to the reading of what may profit him."[1]   And in reference to his First Volume he says : " My sole drift is to be useful ; a point which, however, I know I should in vain aim at unless I could be likewise entertaining. . . My readers will hardly have begun to laugh before they will be called upon to correct that levity, and peruse me with a more serious air."[2] In the shorter poems too this end is aimed at by the moral or religious lessons or reflections with which so many of them close ; as, for example, in the case of *A Fable, The Nightingale and the Glow-Worm*, and *The Dog and the Water-Lily* ; while a similar didactic strain is diffused through others, such as *Alexander Selkirk* and *Heroism* ; and we cannot read even the slighter pieces which make up the present volume without feeling that the author is true to the character which he gives himself :—

> " I, who scribble rhyme
> To catch the triflers of the time,
> And tell them truths divine and clear,
> Which, couched in prose, they will not hear."[3]

Cowper's
Style :
(a) Its Simpli-
city ;

Among the chief qualities of Cowper's style, the most remarkable perhaps is its Simplicity. His acknowledged aim was not to court popularity but to do good, and accordingly he delivers his message with

---

[1] *Letters, To Newton*, Nov. 27, 1784.
[2] *Ib., To Mrs. Cowper*, Oct. 19, 1781.
[3] *A Poetical Epistle to Lady Austen*, 19-22.

a sincere directness that goes straight to the point. It is, for instance, to this unadorned simplicity and directness that his noble ode *On the loss of the Royal George* owes its pathos and its power. He has an abhorrence of affectation of any kind, and is filled with too much earnestness of purpose to leave room for any air of pretentiousness or mysticism. In his language he is plain and outspoken, but never coarse; and it is this genuineness of the man that invests his writings with moral dignity as well as with literary excellence.

In one point, however, he falls short of his usual simplicity—in his fondness for long, Latin derivatives, such as, in the *Task*, *prolixity* (i. 265), *ostentatious* (iii. 420), *ebriety* (iv. 460), *tramontane* (*ib.* 533), *supplemental* (*ib.* 769), *unequivocal* (v. 653); and in his shorter poems, *conflagration* (*Heroism*, 12), *voluminous* (*ib.* 15), *confectionary* (*Mother's Picture*, 61), *impregnated* (*ib.* 94). But in these latter pieces this characteristic is much less prominent than in the longer and more didactic poems. These expressions and others like them we can set down to the scholar's predilection for classical phraseology, and still more to the taste for a Latinized style that was so common in Cowper's time under the literary influence of Dr. Johnson; but when we meet with such mouth-filling polysyllables as *vertiginous* (*Task*, ii. 102), *oscitancy* (*ib.* ii. 774), and *stercoraceous* (*ib.* iii. 463), we are more puzzled, and half wonder whether our author is not making fun of his readers. Cowper also, like Milton, not infrequently uses words in their primitive Latin sense, as *soliciting* (*Task*, iii. 115), *expatiate* (*ib.* iv. 107), *resulting* (*ib.* v. 802), *admiring* (*The Needless Alarm*, 49), and *involved* (*The Castaway*, 1);

though sometimes long-worded and Latinised; traces of artificiality and commonplace.

and though he is for the most part emancipated from
the conventional style of the Artificial School, we find
occasional traces of it in his writings, as in his
use, for instance, of "fragrant lymph"[1] for "tea," and
of "levelled tube"[2] for "gun," which are Pope all
over.[3] Occasionally, too, his simplicity degenerates
into commonplace, especially when he is moralising,
and he descends into such metrical prose as the
following :—

> " Arms, through the vanity and brainless rage
>   Of those that bear them, in whatever cause,
>   *Seem most at variance with all moral good,*
>   *And incompatible with serious thought.*"[4]

The next quality is Perspicuity. Cowper is as clear
and distinct in his thoughts as he is in their expression. His language and his conceptions are so free
from ambiguities that we are never at a loss for his
meaning. He enunciates his own views on this point
in his advice to a young kinsman of his who had
ventured on a poem: "Remember that, in writing,
perspicuity is always more than half the battle. The
want of it is the ruin of more than half the poetry
that is published. A meaning that does not stare
you in the face is as bad as no meaning, because
nobody will take the pains to poke for it."[5] This
statement of the case is perhaps somewhat too sweep-
ing; but the fact remains that Cowper followed this
principle in his own practice, and this transparency of

---

[1] *Task*, iii. 391.   [2] *Hope*, 350.
[3] See also notes, p. 96, l. 1 ; p. 112, l. 71.   [4] *Task*, iv. 619-622.
[5] *Letters*, *To John Johnson*, Feb. 28, 1790.

style is one of the characteristics that make his poems so admirable as a class-book.

Another quality that Cowper claims for himself is Originality. "I reckon it," he writes, "among my principal advantages, as a composer of verses, that I have not read an English poet these thirteen years, and but one these twenty years. Imitation, even of the best models, is my aversion; it is servile and mechanical, a trick that has enabled many to usurp the name of author, who could not have written at all, if they had not written upon the pattern of somebody indeed original."[1] And again: "My delineations of the heart are from my own experience: not one of them borrowed from books, or in the least degree conjectural. In my numbers . . . I have imitated nobody, though sometimes perhaps there may be an apparent resemblance; because at the same time that I would not imitate, I have not affectedly differed."[2] That Cowper has made good this claim may well be conceded; he had too much independence of character to become a copyist of others. At the same time there are obvious resemblances to Pope in the Moral Satires; and in the Task, both as regards rhythm and phraseology, he is to some extent indebted to Milton. We find, too, occasional reminiscences of Gray in his writings.[3] He owes still more to the influence of Thomson, one of the leaders in the return from conventionalism to nature, whom he himself char-

(c) Its Originality.

---

[1] *Letters, To Unwin,* Nov. 24, 1781.
[2] *Ib., To Unwin,* Oct. 10, 1784.
[3] See notes, p. 72, l. 38; p. 78, l. 7; p. 80, l. 34.

c

acterises as "admirable in description" and as "a true poet."[1]

(d) Its Descriptive Power.

We pass on to Cowper's wonderful Descriptive Power. Such is the sensibility of his mind that every detail of a scene is mirrored upon it with the minutest fidelity, as upon the sensitive plate of a photographic camera. In this power he reminds us of Homer; and the secret of it is that he describes what he knows and has seen with his own eyes. The poets of the Pope school never really studied nature for themselves, and so were compelled to piece out their descriptions with stock epithets and artificial phrases. "My descriptions," writes Cowper, and he writes truly, "are all from nature: not one of them second-handed."[2] Hence we find in them an absence of vagueness, of loose and inaccurate generalities; and, instead, that almost scientific accuracy which is so marked a feature in the modern style of poetry.[3] If, when he moralises, he is sometimes commonplace, he is never so when he describes; and it is to the wonderful skill and consummate truth of his pictures, whether of nature or of humanity, more than to anything else, that he owes his high rank among English poets. The description of the woodman and his dog in "The Winter Morning Walk"[4] is an admirable example of this pictorial effectiveness. Note especially the lines—

---

[1] *Letters, To Mrs. King*, June 19, 1788.
[2] *Ib., To Unwin*, Oct. 10, 1784.
[3] See W. J. Dawson's *Makers of Modern English*, pp. 12, 13.
[4] Ll. 41-57.

" His dog attends him. Close behind his heel
    Now creeps he slow ; and now with many a frisk
    Wide scampering, snatches up the drifted snow
    With ivory teeth, or ploughs it with his snout ;
    Then shakes his powdered coat, and barks for joy."

In this book, *The Needless Alarm*, *The Dog and the Water-Lily*, and *The Castaway* are specially remarkable for their descriptive power.

We may notice finally Cowper's Subjectivity. He (*c*) Its Subjec-tivity. is himself a part of what he tells, and the fact that his compositions are full of the poet himself forms one of their special charms. These personal touches are introduced so naively and naturally into his verse, that it never occurs to us to charge him with vanity or self-consciousness. He seems to take his readers into his confidence, as if they were his personal friends, and to wish them to share in and sympathise with his thoughts and feelings, his likes and dislikes, his adventures and surroundings. His shorter poems, in-deed, as has been pointed out already, are in a great part made up of his own doings and experiences ; and from the materials to be found in this one volume it would not be difficult to build up an instructive sketch of the author's habits and character.

A FABLE.

A RAVEN, while with glossy breast
Her new-laid eggs she fondly pressed,
And, on her wicker-work high mounted,
Her chickens prematurely counted,
(A fault philosophers might blame,   5
If quite exempted from the same),
Enjoyed at ease the genial day ;
'Twas April, as the bumpkins say,
The legislature called it May.
But suddenly a wind, as high   10
As ever swept a winter sky,
Shook the young leaves about her ears,
And filled her with a thousand fears,
Lest the rude blast should snap the bough,
And spread her golden hopes below.   15
But just at eve the blowing weather
And all her fears were hushed together ;
"And now," quoth poor unthinking Ralph,
" 'Tis over, and the brood is safe ; "
(For ravens, though, as birds of omen,   20
They teach both conjurers and old women
To tell us what is to befall,
Can't prophesy themselves at all).

C

The morning came, when neighbour Hodge,
Who long had marked her airy lodge,   25
And destined all the treasure there
A gift to his expecting fair,
Climbed like a squirrel to his dray,
And bore the worthless prize away.

MORAL.

'Tis Providence alone secures   30
In every change both mine and yours :
Safety consists not in escape
From dangers of a frightful shape ;
An earthquake may be bid to spare
The man that's strangled by a hair.   35
Fate steals along with silent tread,
Found oftenest in what least we dread,
Frowns in the storm with angry brow,
But in the sunshine strikes the blow.

A COMPARISON.

The lapse of time and rivers is the same,
Both speed their journey with a restless stream ;
The silent pace with which they steal away.
No wealth can bribe, no prayers persuade to stay ;
Alike irrevocable both when past,   5
And a wide ocean swallows both at last.
Though each resemble each in every part,
A difference strikes at length the musing heart ;
Streams never flow in vain ; where streams abound
How laughs the land with various plenty crowned !   10
But time, that should enrich the nobler mind,
Neglected, leaves a dreary waste behind.

ANOTHER.

ADDRESSED TO A YOUNG LADY.

Sweet stream, that winds through yonder glade,
Apt emblem of a virtuous maid !
Silent and chaste she steals along,
Far from the world's gay busy throng,
With gentle yet prevailing force,   5
Intent upon her destined course ;
Graceful and useful all she does,
Blessing and blessed where'er she goes ;
Pure-bosomed as that watery glass,
And heaven reflected in her face !   10

VERSES

SUPPOSED TO BE WRITTEN BY ALEXANDER SELKIRK
DURING HIS SOLITARY ABODE ON THE ISLAND OF
JUAN FERNANDEZ.

I am monarch of all I survey,
  My right there is none to dispute,
From the centre all round to the sea,
  I am lord of the fowl and the brute.
O Solitude ! where are the charms   5
  That sages have seen in thy face ?
Better dwell in the midst of alarms,
  Than reign in this horrible place.

I am out of humanity's reach,
  I must finish my journey alone,   10
Never hear the sweet music of speech,
  I start at the sound of my own.
The beasts that roam over the plain,
  My form with indifference see ;
They are so unacquainted with man,   15
  Their tameness is shocking to me.

Society, friendship, and love,
   Divinely bestowed upon man,
Oh, had I the wings of a dove,
   How soon would I taste you again !   20
My sorrows I then might assuage
   In the ways of religion and truth,
Might learn from the wisdom of age,
   And be cheered by the sallies of youth.

Religion ! what treasure untold   25
   Resides in that heavenly word !
More precious than silver and gold,
   Or all that this earth can afford.
But the sound of the church-going bell
   These valleys and rocks never heard,   30
Never sighed at the sound of a knell,
   Or smiled when a sabbath appeared.

Ye winds, that have made me your sport,
   Convey to this desolate shore
Some cordial endearing report   35
   Of a land I shall visit no more.
My friends,—do they now and then send
   A wish or a thought after me ?
O tell me I yet have a friend,
   Though a friend I am never to see.   40

How fleet is a glance of the mind !
   Compared with the speed of its flight,
The tempest itself lags behind,
   And the swift-wingèd arrows of light.
When I think of my own native land,   45
   In a moment I seem to be there ;
But alas ! recollection at hand
   Soon hurries me back to despair.

But the sea-fowl is gone to her nest,
   The beast is laid down in his lair,   50

Even here is a season of rest,
  And I to my cabin repair.
There's mercy in every place,
  And mercy, encouraging thought !
Gives even affliction a grace,   55
  And reconciles man to his lot.

REPORT OF AN ADJUDGED CASE.

NOT TO BE FOUND IN ANY OF THE BOOKS.

BETWEEN Nose and Eyes a strange contest arose,
  The spectacles set them unhappily wrong ;
The point in dispute was, as all the world knows,
  To which the said spectacles ought to belong.

So Tongue was the lawyer, and argued the cause   5
  With a great deal of skill, and a wig full of learning ;
While Chief Baron Ear sat to balance the laws,
  So famed for his talent in nicely discerning.

" In behalf of the Nose it will quickly appear,
  And your lordship," he said, " will undoubtedly find, 10
That the Nose has had spectacles always in wear,
  Which amounts to possession time out of mind."

Then holding the spectacles up to the court—
  " Your lordship observes they are made with a straddle,
As wide as the ridge of the Nose is ; in short,   15
  Designed to sit close to it, just like a saddle.

" Again, would your lordship a moment suppose
  ('Tis a case that has happened, and may be again)
That the visage or countenance had not a Nose,
  Pray who would, or who could, wear spectacles then ? 20

" On the whole it appears, and my argument shows,
  With a reasoning the court will never condemn,

That the spectacles plainly were made for the Nose,
   And the Nose was as plainly intended for them."

Then shifting his side, as a lawyer knows how,   25
   He pleaded again in behalf of the Eyes :
But what were his arguments few people know,
   For the court did not think they were equally wise.

So his lordship decreed with a grave solemn tone,
   Decisive and clear, without one *if* or *but*—   30
That, whenever the Nose put his spectacles on,
   By daylight or candlelight—Eyes should be shut !

THE LILY AND THE ROSE.

THE nymph must lose her female friend
   If more admired than she—
But where will fierce contention end,
   If flowers can disagree ?

Within the garden's peaceful scene   5
   Appeared two lovely foes,
Aspiring to the rank of Queen,
   The Lily and the Rose.

The Rose soon reddened into rage,
   And, swelling with disdain,   10
Appealed to many a poet's page
   To prove her right to reign.

The Lily's height bespoke command,
   A fair imperial flower ;
She seemed designed for Flora's hand,   15
   The sceptre of her power.

This civil bickering and debate
   The goddess chanced to hear,
And flew to save, ere yet too late,
   The pride of the parterre.   20

Yours is, she said, the noblest hue,
    And yours the statelier mien ;
And, till a third surpasses you,
    Let each be deemed a queen.

Thus soothed and reconciled, each seeks   25
    The fairest British fair ;
The seat of empire is her cheeks,
    They reign united there.

THE NIGHTINGALE AND THE GLOW-WORM.

A NIGHTINGALE, that all day long
Had cheered the village with his song,
Nor yet at eve his note suspended,
Nor yet when eventide was ended,
Began to feel, as well he might,   5
The keen demands of appetite ;
When, looking eagerly around,
He spied far off, upon the ground,
A something shining in the dark,
And knew the glow-worm by his spark ;   10
So stooping down from hawthorn top,
He thought to put him in his crop.
The worm, aware of his intent,
Harangued him thus, right eloquent :
    " Did you admire my lamp," quoth he,   15
" As much as I your minstrelsy,   .
You would abhor to do me wrong,
As much as I to spoil your song ;
For 'twas the self-same Power divine
Taught you to sing and me to shine ;   20
That you with music, I with light,
Might beautify and cheer the night."

The songster heard his short oration,
And, warbling out his approbation,
Released him, as my story tells,   25
And found a supper somewhere else.
  Hence jarring sectaries may learn
Their real interest to discern ;
That brother should not war with brother,
And worry and devour each other ;   30
But sing and shine by sweet consent,
Till life's poor transient night is spent,
Respecting, in each other's case,
The gifts of nature and of grace.
  Those Christians best deserve the name   35
Who studiously make peace their aim ;
Peace both the duty and the prize
Of him that creeps and him that flies.

ON A GOLDFINCH STARVED TO DEATH
IN HIS CAGE.

TIME was when I was free as air,
The thistle's downy seed my fare,
  My drink the morning dew ;
I perched at will on every spray,
My form genteel, my plumage gay,   5
  My strains for ever new.

But gaudy plumage, sprightly strain,
And form genteel were all in vain,
  And of a transient date ;
For, caught and caged and starved to death,   10
In dying sighs my little breath
  Soon passed the wiry grate.

Thanks, gentle swain, for all my woes,
And thanks for this effectual close
  And cure of every ill !   15
More cruelty could none express ;
And I, if you had shown me less,
  Had been your prisoner still.

THE PINEAPPLE AND THE BEE.

The Pineapples, in triple row,
Were basking hot, and all in blow ;
A Bee of most discerning taste
Perceived the fragrance as he passed ;
On eager wing the spoiler came,   5
And searched for crannies in the frame,
Urged his attempt on every side,
To every pane his trunk applied ;
But still in vain, the frame was tight,
And only pervious to the light ;   10
Thus having wasted half the day,
He trimmed his flight another way.
  " Methinks," I said, " in thee I find
The sin and madness of mankind.
To joys forbidden man aspires,   15
Consumes his soul with vain desires ;
Folly the spring of his pursuit,
And disappointment all the fruit.
While Cynthio ogles as she passes,
The nymph between two chariot glasses,   20
She is the Pineapple, and he
The silly unsuccessful Bee.
The maid who views with pensive air
The showglass fraught with glittering ware,
Sees watches, bracelets, rings, and lockets,   25
But sighs at thought of empty pockets ;

Like thine, her appetite is keen,
But ah, the cruel glass between !"
Our dear delights are often such,
Exposed to view, but not to touch ;   30
The sight our foolish heart inflames,
We long for pineapples in frames;
With hopeless wish one looks and lingers :
One breaks the glass, and cuts his fingers ;
But they whom Truth and Wisdom lead,   35
Can gather honey from a weed.

THE JACKDAW.

THERE is a bird who by his coat,
And by the hoarseness of his note,
  Might be supposed a crow ;
A great frequenter of the church,
Where bishop-like he finds a perch,   5
  And dormitory too.

Above the steeple shines a plate,
That turns and turns, to indicate
  From what point blows the weather ;
Look up—your brains begin to swim,   10
'Tis in the clouds—that pleases him,
  He chooses it the rather.

Fond of the speculative height,
Thither he wings his airy flight,
  And thence securely sees   15
The bustle and the raree-show
That occupy mankind below,
  Secure and at his ease.

You think, no doubt, he sits and muses
On future broken bones and bruises,   20
  If he should chance to fall.

No ; not a single thought like that
Employs his philosophic pate,
   Or troubles it at all.

He sees that this great roundabout,   25
The world, with all its motley rout,
   Church, army, physic, law,
Its customs, and its businesses,
Are no concern at all of his,
   And says—what says he ?—" Caw."   30

Thrice happy bird ! I too have seen
Much of the vanities of men ;
   And sick of having seen 'em,
Would cheerfully these limbs resign
For such a pair of wings as thine,   35
   And such a head between 'em.

THE CRICKET.

LITTLE inmate, full of mirth,
Chirping on my kitchen hearth,
Wheresoe'er be thine abode,
Always harbinger of good,
Pay me for thy warm retreat   5
With a song more soft and sweet ;
In return thou shalt receive
Such a strain as I can give.

Thus thy praise shall be expressed,
Inoffensive, welcome guest !   10
While the rat is on the scout,
And the mouse with curious snout,
With what vermin else infest
Every dish, and spoil the best ;
Frisking thus before the fire,   15
Thou hast all thine heart's desire.

Though in voice and shape they be
Formed as if akin to thee,
Thou surpassest, happier far,
Happiest grasshoppers that are ;　　　　　20
Theirs is but a summer's song,
Thine endures the winter long,
Unimpaired, and shrill, and clear,
Melody throughout the year.

Neither night, nor dawn of day,　　　　　25
Puts a period to thy play ;
Sing then—and extend thy span
Far beyond the date of man.
Wretched man, whose years are spent
In repining discontent,　　　　　30
Lives not, aged though he be,
Half a span compared with thee.

BOADICEA.

When the British warrior queen,
　　Bleeding from the Roman rods,
Sought, with an indignant mien,
　　Counsel of her country's gods,

Sage beneath a spreading oak　　　　　5
　　Sat the Druid, hoary chief,
Every burning word he spoke
　　Full of rage and full of grief :

" Princess ! if our aged eyes
　　Weep upon thy matchless wrongs,　　　10
'Tis because resentment ties
　　All the terrors of our tongues.

" Rome shall perish—write that word
　　In the blood that she has spilt ;

Perish hopeless and abhorred,   15
   Deep in ruin as in guilt.

"Rome, for empire far renowned,
   Tramples on a thousand states;
Soon her pride shall kiss the ground,—
   Hark! the Gaul is at her gates.   20

"Other Romans shall arise,
   Heedless of a soldier's name,
Sounds, not arms, shall win the prize,
   Harmony the path to fame.

"Then the progeny that springs   25
   From the forests of our land,
Armed with thunder, clad with wings,
   Shall a wider world command.

"Regions Cæsar never knew
   Thy posterity shall sway,   30
Where his eagles never flew,
   None invincible as they."

Such the bard's prophetic words,
   Pregnant with celestial fire,
Bending as he swept the chords   35
   Of his sweet but awful lyre.

She, with all a monarch's pride,
   Felt them in her bosom glow,
Rushed to battle, fought and died;
   Dying, hurled them at the foe.   40

"Ruffians, pitiless as proud,
   Heaven awards the vengeance due;
Empire is on us bestowed,
   Shame and ruin wait for you!"

HEROISM.

THERE was a time when Ætna's silent fire
Slept unperceived, the mountain yet entire ;
When, conscious of no danger from below,
She towered a cloud-capt pyramid of snow.
No thunders shook with deep intestine sound   5
The blooming groves that girdled her around ;
Her unctuous olives and her purple vines,
(Unfelt the fury of those bursting mines)
The peasant's hopes, and not in vain, assured,
In peace upon her sloping sides matured.   10
When on a day, like that of the last doom,
A conflagration labouring in her womb,
She teemed and heaved with an infernal birth,
That shook the circling seas and solid earth.
Dark and voluminous the vapours rise,   15
And hang their horrors in the neigbouring skies,
While through the Stygian veil that blots the day
In dazzling streaks the livid lightnings play.
But oh ! what muse, and in what powers of song,
Can trace the torrent as it burns along ?   20
Havoc and devastation in the van,
It marches o'er the prostrate works of man,
Vines, olives, herbage, forests disappear,
And all the charms of a Sicilian year.

Revolving seasons, fruitless as they pass,   25
See it an uninformed and idle mass,
Without a soil to invite the tiller's care,
Or blade that might redeem it from despair.
Yet time at length (what will not time achieve ?)
Clothes it with earth, and bids the produce live.   30
Once more the spiry myrtle crowns the glade,
And ruminating flocks enjoy the shade.
O bliss precarious, and unsafe retreats !
O charming paradise of short-lived sweets !

The self-same gale that wafts the fragrance round   35
Brings to the distant ear a sullen sound :
Again the mountain feels the imprisoned foe,
Again pours ruin on the vale below,
Ten thousand swains the wasted scene deplore,
That only future ages can restore.   40

Ye monarchs, whom the lure of honour draws,
Who write in blood the merits of your cause,
Who strike the blow, then plead your own defence,
Glory your aim, but Justice your pretence,
Behold in Ætna's emblematic fires   45
The mischiefs your ambitious pride inspires !

Fast by the stream that bounds your just domain,
And tells you where you have a right to reign,
A nation dwells, not envious of your throne,
Studious of peace, their neighbours' and their own.   50
Ill-fated race ! how deeply must they rue
Their only crime, vicinity to you !
The trumpet sounds, your legions swarm abroad,
Through the ripe harvest lies their destined road,
At every step beneath their feet they tread   55
The life of multitudes, a nation's bread !
Earth seems a garden in its loveliest dress
Before them, and behind a wilderness ;
Famine, and Pestilence her first-born son,
Attend to finish what the sword begun ;   60
And echoing praises such as fiends might earn
And folly pays, resound at your return.
A calm succeeds ; but Plenty, with her train
Of heartfelt joys, succeeds not soon again,
And years of pining indigence must show   65
What scourges are the gods that rule below.

Yet man, laborious man, by slow degrees,
(Such is his thirst of opulence and ease)

Plies all the sinews of industrious toil,
Gleans up the refuse of the general spoil,   70
Rebuilds the towers that smoked upon the plain,
And the sun gilds the shining spires again.

Increasing commerce and reviving art
Renew the quarrel on the conqueror's part ;
And the sad lesson must be learned once more,   75
That wealth within is ruin at the door.

What are ye, monarchs, laurelled heroes, say,
But Ætnas of the suffering world ye sway ?
Sweet Nature, stripped of her embroidered robe,
Deplores the wasted regions of her globe,   80
And stands a witness at Truth's awful bar,
To prove you there destroyers, as ye are.

Oh place me in some heaven-protected isle,
Where peace and equity and freedom smile,
Where no volcano pours his fiery flood,   85
No crested warrior dips his plume in blood,
Where power secures what industry has won,
Where to succeed is not to be undone,
A land that distant tyrants hate in vain,
In Britain's isle, beneath a George's reign.   90

AN EPISTLE TO JOSEPH HILL.

DEAR JOSEPH,—Five and twenty years ago—
Alas, how time escapes !—'tis even so—
With frequent intercourse, and always sweet,
And always friendly, we were wont to cheat
A tedious hour, and now we never meet !   5
As some grave gentleman in Terence says
('Twas therefore much the same in ancient days),
Good lack, we know not what to-morrow brings—
Strange fluctuation of all human things !

True. Changes will befall, and friends may part,   10
But distance only cannot change the heart :
And were I called to prove the assertion true,
One proof should serve—a reference to you.
 Whence comes it, then, that in the wane of life,
Though nothing have occurred to kindle strife,   15
We find the friends we fancied we had won,
Though numerous once, reduced to few or none ?
Can gold grow worthless, that has stood the touch ?
No ; gold they seemed, but they were never such.
 Horatio's servant once, with bow and cringe,   20
Swinging the parlour door upon its hinge,
Dreading a negative, and overawed
Lest he should trespass, begged to go abroad.
"Go, fellow !—whither ?"—turning short about—
" Nay. Stay at home—you're always going out."—   25
" 'Tis but a step, sir ; just at the street's end."—
" For what ?"—" An please you, sir, to see a friend."—
" A friend !" Horatio cried, and seemed to start—
" Yea marry shalt thou, and with all my heart.
And fetch my cloak ; for, though the night be raw,   30
I'll see him too—the first I ever saw."
 I knew the man, and knew his nature mild,
And was his plaything often when a child ;
But somewhat at that moment pinched him close,
Else he was seldom bitter or morose.   35
Perhaps, his confidence just then betrayed,
His grief might prompt him with the speech he made ;
Perhaps 'twas mere good humour gave it birth,
The harmless play of pleasantry and mirth.
Howe'er it was, his language, in my mind,   40
Bespoke at least a man that knew mankind.
 But not to moralize too much, and strain
To prove an evil of which all complain,
(I hate long arguments verbosely spun)
One story more, dear Hill, and I have done.   45

Once on a time, an emperor, a wise man,
No matter where, in China or Japan,
Decreed, that whosoever should offend
Against the well-known duties of a friend,
Convicted once, should ever after wear   50
But half a coat, and show his bosom bare :
The punishment importing this, no doubt,
That all was naught within, and all found out.
  O happy Britain ! we have not to fear
Such hard and arbitrary measure here ;   55
Else, could a law like that which I relate
Once have the sanction of our triple state,
Some few that I have known in days of old,
Would run most dreadful risk of catching cold ;
While you, my friend, whatever wind should blow,   60
Might traverse England safely to and fro,
An honest man, close buttoned to the chin,
Broadcloth without, and a warm heart within.

THE DIVERTING HISTORY OF JOHN GILPIN.

SHOWING HOW HE WENT FARTHER THAN HE INTENDED AND CAME SAFE HOME AGAIN.

JOHN GILPIN was a citizen
  Of credit and renown,
A train-band captain eke was he
  Of famous London Town.

John Gilpin's spouse said to her dear,   5
  "Though wedded we have been
These twice ten tedious years, yet we
  No holiday have seen.

"To-morrow is our wedding-day,
  And we will then repair   10

Unto the Bell at Edmonton,
  All in a chaise and pair.

"My sister, and my sister's child,
  Myself, and children three,
Will fill the chaise ; so you must ride   15
  On horseback after we."

He soon replied, "I do admire
  Of womankind but one,
And you are she, my dearest dear,
  Therefore it shall be done.   20

"I am a linen-draper bold,
  As all the world doth know,
And my good friend the calender
  Will lend his horse to go."

Quoth Mrs. Gilpin, "That's well said ;   25
  And for that wine is dear,
We will be furnished with our own,
  Which is both bright and clear."

John Gilpin kissed his loving wife ;
  O'erjoyed was he to find,   30
That though on pleasure she was bent,
  She had a frugal mind.

The morning came, the chaise was brought,
  But yet was not allowed
To drive up to the door, lest all   35
  Should say that she was proud.

So three doors off the chaise was stayed,
  Where they did all get in ;
Six precious souls, and all agog
  To dash through thick and thin.   40

Smack went the whip, round went the wheels,
  Were never folk so glad,

The stones did rattle underneath,
　As if Cheapside were mad.

John Gilpin at his horse's side   45
　Seized fast the flowing mane,
And up he got, in haste to ride,
　But soon came down again ;

For saddle-tree scarce reached had he,
　His journey to begin,   50
When, turning round his head, he saw
　Three customers come in.

So down he came ; for loss of time,
　Although it grieved him sore,
Yet loss of pence, full well he knew,   55
　Would trouble him much more.

'Twas long before the customers
　Were suited to their mind,
When Betty screaming came down stairs,
　"The wine is left behind !"   60

"Good lack !" quoth he—"yet bring it me,
　My leathern belt likewise,
In which I bear my trusty sword,
　When I do exercise."

Now Mistress Gilpin (careful soul !)   65
　Had two stone bottles found,
To hold the liquor that she loved,
　And keep it safe and sound.

Each bottle had a curling ear,
　Through which the belt he drew,   70
And hung a bottle on each side,
　To make his balance true.

Then over all, that he might be
　Equipped from top to toe,

His long red cloak, well brushed and neat,   75
  He manfully did throw.

Now see him mounted once again
  Upon his nimble steed,
Full slowly pacing o'er the stones,
  With caution and good heed.   80

But finding soon a smoother road
  Beneath his well-shod feet,
The snorting beast began to trot,
  Which galled him in his seat.

So, " Fair and softly," John he cried,   85
  But John he cried in vain ;
That trot became a gallop soon,
  In spite of curb and rein.

So stooping down, as needs he must
  Who cannot sit upright,   90
He grasped the mane with both his hands,
  And eke with all his might.

His horse, who never in that sort
  Had handled been before,
What thing upon his back had got   95
  Did wonder more and more.

Away went Gilpin, neck or nought ;
  Away went hat and wig ;
He little dreamt, when he set out,
  Of running such a rig.   100

The wind did blow, the cloak did fly,
  Like streamer long and gay,
Till, loop and button failing both,
  At last it flew away.

Then might all people well discern   105
  The bottles he had slung ;

A bottle swinging at each side,
　　As hath been said or sung.

The dogs did bark, the children screamed,
　　Up flew the windows all ;　　　　　　　110
And every soul cried out, " Well done ! "
　　As loud as he could bawl.

Away went Gilpin—who but he ?
　　His fame soon spread around ;
" He carries weight ! "　" He rides a race ! "　115
　" 'Tis for a thousand pound ! "

And still, as fast as he drew near,
　　'Twas wonderful to view,
How in a trice the turnpike-men
　　Their gates wide open threw.　　　　　120

And now, as he went bowing down
　　His reeking head full low,
The bottles twain behind his back
　　Were shattered at a blow.

Down ran the wine into the road,　　　　125
　　Most piteous to be seen,
Which made his horse's flanks to smoke
　　As they had basted been.

But still he seemed to carry weight,
　　With leathern girdle braced ;　　　　　130
For all might see the bottle-necks
　　Still dangling at his waist.

Thus all through merry Islington
　　These gambols he did play,
Until he came unto the Wash　　　　　　135
　　Of Edmonton so gay ;

And there he threw the Wash about
　　On both sides of the way,

Just like unto a trundling mop,
   Or a wild goose at play.   140

At Edmonton his loving wife
   From the balcony spied
Her tender husband, wondering much
   To see how he did ride.

"Stop, stop, John Gilpin !—Here's the house !"   145
   They all at once did cry ;
"The dinner waits, and we are tired ;"—
   Said Gilpin—"So am I !"

But yet his horse was not a whit
   Inclined to tarry there !   150
For why ?—his owner had a house
   Full ten miles off, at Ware.

So like an arrow swift he flew,
   Shot by an archer strong ;
So did he fly—which brings me to   155
   The middle of my song.

Away went Gilpin, out of breath,
   And sore against his will,
Till at his friend the calender's
   His horse at last stood still.   160

The calender, amazed to see
   His neighbour in such trim,
Laid down his pipe, flew to the gate,
   And thus accosted him :

"What news ? what news ? your tidings tell ;   165
   Tell me you must and shall—
Say why bareheaded you are come,
   Or why you come at all ?"

Now Gilpin had a pleasant wit,
   And loved a timely joke ;   170

And thus unto the calender
  In merry guise he spoke :

" I came because your horse would come,
  And, if I well forebode,
My hat and wig will soon be here—   175
  They are upon the road."

The calender, right glad to find
  His friend in merry pin,
Returned him not a single word,
  But to the house went in ;   180

Whence straight he came with hat and wig ;
  A wig that flowed behind,
A hat not much the worse for wear,
  Each comely in its kind.

He held them up, and in his turn   185
  Thus showed his ready wit,
" My head is twice as big as yours,
  They therefore needs must fit.

" But let me scrape the dirt away
  That hangs upon your face ;   190
And stop and eat, for well you may
  Be in a hungry case."

Said John, " It is my wedding-day,
  And all the world would stare,
If wife should dine at Edmonton,   195
  And I should dine at Ware."

So turning to his horse, he said,
  " I am in haste to dine ;
'Twas for your pleasure you came here,
  You shall go back for mine."   200

Ah, luckless speech, and bootless boast !
  For which he paid full dear ;

For, while he spake, a braying ass
    Did sing most loud and clear;

Whereat his horse did snort, as he   205
    Had heard a lion roar,
And galloped off with all his might,
    As he had done before.

Away went Gilpin, and away
    Went Gilpin's hat and wig: 210
He lost them sooner than at first;
    For why?—they were too big.

Now Mistress Gilpin, when she saw
    Her husband posting down
Into the country far away,   215
    She pulled out half-a-crown;

And thus unto the youth she said
    That drove them to the Bell,
'This shall be yours, when you bring back
    My husband safe and well."   220

The youth did ride, and soon did meet
    John coming back amain:
Whom in a trice he tried to stop,
    By catching at his rein;

But not performing what he meant,   225
    And gladly would have done,
The frighted steed he frighted more,
    And made him faster run.

Away went Gilpin, and away
    Went postboy at his heels,   230
The postboy's horse right glad to miss
    The lumbering of the wheels.

Six gentlemen upon the road,
    Thus seeing Gilpin fly,

With postboy scampering in the rear,   235
  They raised the hue and cry :

"Stop thief ! stop thief !—a highwayman !"
  Not one of them was mute ;
And all and each that passed that way
  Did join in the pursuit.   240

And now the turnpike gates again
  Flew open in short space ;
The toll-men thinking, as before,
  That Gilpin rode a race.

And so he did, and won it too,   245
  For he got first to town ;
Nor stopped till where he had got up
  He did again get down.

Now let us sing, Long live the king !
  And Gilpin, long live he !   250
And when he next doth ride abroad
  May I be there to see !

THE POPLAR FIELD.

The poplars are felled ; farewell to the shade,
And the whispering sound of the cool colonnade,
The winds play no longer and sing in the leaves,
Nor Ouse on his bosom their image receives.

Twelve years have elapsed since I first took a view   5
Of my favourite field, and the bank where they grew ;
And now in the grass behold they are laid,
And the tree is my seat that once lent me a shade !

The blackbird has fled to another retreat,
Where the hazels afford him a screen from the heat, 10
And the scene where his melody charmed me before
Resounds with his sweet-flowing ditty no more.

My fugitive years are all hasting away,
And I must ere long lie as lowly as they,
With a turf on my breast, and a stone at my head,   15
Ere another such grove shall arise in its stead.

'Tis a sight to engage me, if anything can,
To muse on the perishing pleasures of man ;
Though his life be a dream, his enjoyments, I see,
Have a being less durable even than he.*   20

THE ROSE.

THE rose had been washed, just washed in a shower,
 Which Mary to Anna conveyed,
The plentiful moisture encumbered the flower,
 And weighed down its beautiful head.

The cup was all filled, and the leaves were all wet,   5
 And it seemed, to a fanciful view,
To weep for the buds it had left with regret
 On the flourishing bush where it grew.

I hastily seized it, unfit as it was
 For a nosegay, so dripping and drowned ;   10
And swinging it rudely, too rudely, alas !
 I snapped it—it fell to the ground.

" And such," I exclaimed, " is the pitiless part
 Some act by the delicate mind,
Regardless of wringing and breaking a heart   15
 Already to sorrow resigned !

* *Note to Ed. of* 1803. Mr. Cowper afterwards altered this last
stanza in the following manner :

> The change both my heart and my fancy employs,
> I reflect on the frailty of man and his joys ;
> Short-lived as we are, yet our pleasures, we see,
> Have a still shorter date, and die sooner than we.

"This elegant rose, had I shaken it less,
  Might have bloomed with its owner awhile;
And the tear that is wiped with a little address
  May be followed perhaps by a smile."   20

ON THE DEATH OF
MRS. THROCKMORTON'S BULLFINCH.

YE Nymphs, if e'er your eyes were red
With tears o'er hapless favourites shed,
    Oh share Maria's grief!
Her favourite, even in his cage
(What will not hunger's cruel rage?)   5
    Assassined by a thief.

Where Rhenus strays his vines among
The egg was laid from which he sprung;
    And though by nature mute,
Or only with a whistle blessed,   10
Well-taught, he all the sounds expressed
    Of flageolet or flute.

The honours of his ebon poll
Were brighter than the sleekest mole,
    His bosom of the hue   15
With which Aurora decks the skies,
When piping winds shall soon arise
    To sweep away the dew.

Above, below, in all the house,
Dire foe alike of bird and mouse,   20
    No cat had leave to dwell;
And Bully's cage supported stood
On props of smoothest-shaven wood,
    Large-built and latticed well.

Well latticed,—but the grate, alas !   25
Not rough with wire of steel or brass,
      For Bully's plumage sake,
But smooth with wands from Ouse's side,
With which, when neatly peeled and dried,
      The swains their baskets make.   30

Night veiled the pole ; all seemed secure ;
When, led by instinct sharp and sure,
      Subsistence to provide,
A beast forth sallied on the scout,
Long-backed, long-tailed, with whiskered snout,   35
      And badger-coloured hide.

He, entering at the study door,
Its ample area 'gan explore ;
      And something in the wind
Conjectured, sniffing round and round,   40
Better than all the books he found,
      Food chiefly for the mind.

Just then, by adverse fate impressed,
A dream disturbed poor Bully's rest ;
      In sleep he seemed to view   45
A rat fast clinging to the cage,
And screaming at the sad presage,
      Awoke and found it true.

For, aided both by ear and scent,
Right to his mark the monster went—   50
      Ah, Muse ! forbear to speak
Minute the horrors that ensued ;
His teeth were strong, the cage was wood—
      He left poor Bully's beak.

Oh, had he made that too his prey !   55
That beak, whence issued many a lay
      Of such mellifluous tone,

E

Might have repaid him well, I wote,
For silencing so sweet a throat,
   Fast stuck within his own.   60

Maria weeps,—the Muses mourn ;—
So, when by Bacchanalians torn,
   On Thracian Hebrus' side
The tree-enchanter Orpheus fell,
His head alone remained to tell   65
   The cruel death he died.

ODE TO APOLLO.

ON AN INK-GLASS ALMOST DRIED IN THE SUN.

PATRON of all those luckless brains
   That, to the wrong side leaning,
Indite much metre with much pains,
   And little or no meaning :

Ah why, since oceans, rivers, streams,   5
   That water all the nations,
Pay tribute to thy glorious beams,
   In constant exhalations ;

Why, stooping from the noon of day,
   Too covetous of drink,   10
Apollo, hast thou stolen away
   A poet's drop of ink ?

Upborne into the viewless air,
   It floats a vapour now,
Impelled through regions dense and rare   15
   By all the winds that blow.

Ordained, perhaps, ere summer flies,
   Combined with millions more,

To form an Iris in the skies,
  Though black and foul before.   20

Illustrious drop ! and happy then
  Beyond the happiest lot,
Of all that ever passed my pen,
  So soon to be forgot !

Phœbus, if such be thy design,   25
  To place it in thy bow,
Give wit, that what is left may shine
  With equal grace below.

THE FAITHFUL BIRD.

THE Greenhouse is my summer seat ;
My shrubs displaced from that retreat
  Enjoyed the open air ;
Two goldfinches, whose sprightly song
· Had been their mutual solace long,   5
  Lived happy prisoners there.

They sang as blithe as finches sing
That flutter loose on golden wing,
  And frolic where they list ;
Strangers to liberty, 'tis true,   10
But that delight they never knew,
  And therefore never missed.

But nature works in every breast,
With force not easily suppressed ;
  And Dick felt some desires,   15
That, after many an effort vain,
Instructed him at length to gain
  A pass between his wires.

The open windows seemed to invite
The freeman to a farewell flight;   20
    But Tom was still confined;
And Dick, although his way was clear,
Was much too generous and sincere
    To leave his friend behind.

So settling on his cage, by play,   25
And chirp, and kiss, he seemed to say,
    "You must not live alone;"—
Nor would he quit that chosen stand
Till I, with slow and cautious hand,
    Returned him to his own.   30

O ye, who never taste the joys
Of friendship, satisfied with noise,
    Fandango, ball, and rout!
Blush when I tell you how a bird
A prison with a friend preferred   35
    To liberty without.

THE NEEDLESS ALARM.

A TALE.

THERE is a field through which I often pass,
Thick overspread with moss, and silky grass,
Adjoining close to Kilwick's echoing wood,
Where oft the bitch-fox hides her hapless brood,
Reserved to solace many a neighbouring squire,   5
That he may follow them through brake and brier,
Contusion hazarding of neck or spine,
Which rural gentlemen call sport divine.
A narrow brook, by rushy banks concealed,
Runs in a bottom, and divides the field;   10
Oaks intersperse it, that had once a head,
But now wear crests of oven-wood instead;

And where the land slopes to its watery bourn
Wide yawns a gulf beside a ragged thorn ;
Bricks line the sides, but shivered long ago,   15
And horrid brambles intertwine below ;
A hollow scooped, I judge, in ancient time,
For baking earth, or burning rock to lime.
    Not yet the hawthorn bore her berries red,
With which the fieldfare, wintry guest, is fed ;   20
Nor Autumn yet had brushed from every spray,
With her chill hand, the mellow leaves away ;
But corn was housed, and beans were in the stack ;
Now therefore issued forth the spotted pack,
With tails high mounted, ears hung low, and throats 25
With a whole gamut filled of heavenly notes,
For which, alas ! my destiny severe,
Though ears she gave me two, gave me no ear.
    The sun, accomplishing his early march,
His lamp now planted on heaven's topmost arch,   30
When, exercise and air my only aim,
And heedless whither, to that field I came,
Ere yet with ruthless joy the happy hound
Told hill and dale that Reynard's track was found,
Or with the high-raised horn's melodious clang   35
All Kilwick and all Dinglederry rang,
    Sheep grazed the field ; some with soft bosom pressed
The herb as soft, while nibbling strayed the rest ;
Nor noise was heard but of the hasty brook,
Struggling, detained in many a petty nook.   40
All seemed so peaceful, that from them conveyed,
To me their peace by kind contagion spread.
    But when the huntsman, with distended cheek,
'Gan make his instrument of music speak,
And from within the wood that crash was heard,   45
Though not a hound from whom it burst appeared,
The sheep recumbent and the sheep that grazed,
All huddling into phalanx, stood and gazed,

Admiring, terrified, the novel strain,   49
Then coursed the field around, and coursed it round again;
But recollecting, with a sudden thought,
That flight in circles urged advanced them nought,
They gathered close around the old pit's brink,
And thought again—but knew not what to think.

   The man to solitude accustomed long   55
Perceives in every thing that lives a tongue ;
Not animals alone, but shrubs and trees
Have speech for him, and understood with ease ;
After long drought, when rains abundant fall,
He hears the herbs and flowers rejoicing all ;   60
Knows what the freshness of their hue implies,
How glad they catch the largess of the skies ;
But, with precision nicer still, the mind
He scans of every locomotive kind ;
Birds of all feather, beasts of every name,   65
That serve mankind or shun them, wild or tame ;
The looks and gestures of their griefs and fears
Have all articulation in his ears ;
He spells them true by intuition's light,
And needs no glossary to set him right.   70

   This truth premised was needful as a text,
To win due credence to what follows next.

   Awhile they mused ; surveying every face,
Thou hadst supposed them of superior race ;
Their periwigs of wool and fears combined   75
Stamped on each countenance such marks of mind,
That sage they seemed, as lawyers o'er a doubt,
Which, puzzling long, at last they puzzle out ;
Or academic tutors, teaching youths,
Sure ne'er to want them, mathematic truths ;   80
When thus a mutton statelier than the rest,
A Ram, the ewes and wethers sad addressed :

   " Friends ! we have lived too long.   I never heard
Sounds such as these, so worthy to be feared.

Could I believe, that winds for ages pent   85
In earth's dark womb have found at last a vent,
And from their prison-house below arise,
With all these hideous howlings to the skies,
I could be much composed, nor should appear,
For such a cause, to feel the slightest fear.   90
Yourselves have seen, what time the thunders rolled
All night, me resting quiet in the fold.
Or heard we that tremendous bray alone,
I could expound the melancholy tone ;
Should deem it by our old companion made,   95
The Ass ; for he, we know, has lately strayed,
And being lost, perhaps, and wandering wide,
Might be supposed to clamour for a guide.
But ah ! those dreadful yells what soul can hear
That owns a carcass, and not quake for fear ?   100
Demons produce them doubtless, brazen-clawed,
And, fanged with brass, the demons are abroad ;
I hold it therefore wisest and most fit
That, life to save, we leap into the pit."

   Him answered then his loving mate and true,   105
But more discreet than he, a Cambrian Ewe :
   "How ! leap into the pit our life to save ?
To save our life leap all into the grave ?
For can we find it less ?   Contemplate first
The depth how awful ! falling there, we burst :   110
Or should the brambles interposed our fall
In part abate, that happiness were small ;
For with a race like theirs no chance I see
Of peace or ease to creatures clad as we.
Meantime, noise kills not.   Be it Dapple's bray,   115
Or be it not, or be it whose it may,
And rush those other sounds, that seem by tongues
Of demons uttered, from whatever lungs,
Sounds are but sounds, and, till the cause appear,
We have at least commodious standing here.   120

Come fiend, come fury, giant, monster, blast
From earth or hell, we can but plunge at last."
    While thus she spake, I fainter heard the peals,
For Reynard, close attended at his heels
By panting dog, tired man, and spattered horse,   125
Through mere good fortune took a different course.
The flock grew calm again, and I, the road
Following, that led me to my own abode,
Much wondered that the silly sheep had found
Such cause of terror in an empty sound,   130
So sweet to huntsman, gentleman, and hound.

MORAL.

Beware of desperate steps. The darkest day,
Live till to-morrow, will have passed away.

THE DOG AND THE WATER-LILY.

NO FABLE.

THE noon was shady, and soft airs
    Swept Ouse's silent tide,
When, 'scaped from literary cares,
    I wandered on his side.

My spaniel, prettiest of his race,   5
    And high in pedigree,
(Two nymphs adorned with every grace
    That spaniel found for me)

Now wantoned, lost in flags and reeds,
    Now starting into sight,   10
Pursued the swallow o'er the meads
    With scarce a slower flight.

It was the time when Ouse displayed
    His lilies newly blown;

Their beauties I intent surveyed   15
  And one I wished my own.

With cane extended far, I sought
  To steer it close to land ;
But still the prize, though nearly caught,
  Escaped my eager hand.   20

Beau marked my unsuccessful pains
  With fixed considerate face,
And puzzling set his puppy brains
  To comprehend the case.

But with a cherup clear and strong   25
  Dispersing all his dream,
I thence withdrew, and followed long
  The windings of the stream.

My ramble ended, I returned ;
  Beau, trotting far before,   30
The floating wreath again discerned,
  And plunging left the shore.

I saw him with that lily cropped
  Impatient swim to meet
My quick approach, and soon he dropped   35
  The treasure at my feet.

Charmed with the sight, "The world," I cried,
  "Shall hear of this thy deed :
My dog shall mortify the pride
  Of man's superior breed :   40

But chief myself I will enjoin,
  Awake at duty's call,
To show a love as prompt as thine
  To Him who gives me all."

ON THE RECEIPT OF MY MOTHER'S PICTURE
OUT OF NORFOLK;

THE GIFT OF MY COUSIN, ANN BODHAM.

On that those lips had language! Life has passed
With me but roughly since I heard thee last.
Those lips are thine—thy own sweet smile I see,
The same that oft in childhood solaced me;
Voice only fails, else how distinct they say,   5
"Grieve not, my child, chase all thy fears away!"
The meek intelligence of those dear eyes
(Blest be the art that can immortalize,
The art that baffles Time's tyrannic claim
To quench it) here shines on me still the same.   10
     Faithful remembrancer of one so dear,
O welcome guest, though unexpected here!
Who bidst me honour with an artless song,
Affectionate, a mother lost so long,
I will obey, not willingly alone,   15
But gladly, as the precept were her own:
And, while that face renews my filial grief,
Fancy shall weave a charm for my relief,
Shall steep me in Elysian reverie,
A momentary dream that thou art she.   20
     My mother! when I learnt that thou wast dead,
Say, wast thou conscious of the tears I shed?
Hovered thy spirit o'er thy sorrowing son,
Wretch even then, life's journey just begun?
Perhaps thou gavest me, though unfelt, a kiss: 25
Perhaps a tear, if souls can weep in bliss—
Ah, that maternal smile! It answers—Yes.
I heard the bell tolled on thy burial day,
I saw the hearse that bore thee slow away,
And, turning from my nursery window, drew   30
A long, long sigh, and wept a last adieu!

But was it such ?—It was.—Where thou art gone
Adieus and farewells are a sound unknown.
May I but meet thee on that peaceful shore,
The parting word shall pass my lips no more !　　35
Thy maidens, grieved themselves at my concern,
Oft gave me promise of thy quick return.
What ardently I wished I long believed,
And, disappointed still, was still deceived ;
By expectation every day beguiled,　　　　40
Dupe of to-morrow even from a child.
Thus many a sad to-morrow came and went,
Till, all my stock of infant sorrow spent,
I learnt at last submission to my lot ;
But, though I less deplored thee, ne'er forgot.　45
　　Where once we dwelt our name is heard no more,
Children not thine have trod my nursery floor ;
And where the gardener Robin, day by day,
Drew me to school along the public way,
Delighted with my bauble coach, and wrapped　50
In scarlet mantle warm, and velvet-capped,
'Tis now become a history little known,
That once we called the pastoral house our own.
Short-lived possession ! but the record fair
That memory keeps, of all thy kindness there,　55
Still outlives many a storm that has effaced
A thousand other themes less deeply traced.
Thy nightly visits to my chamber made,
That thou mightst know me safe and warmly laid ;
Thy morning bounties ere I left my home,　　60
The biscuit, or confectionary plum ;
The fragrant waters on my cheek bestowed
By thy own hand, till fresh they shone and glowed ;
All this, and more endearing still than all,
Thy constant flow of love, that knew no fall,　　65
Ne'er roughened by those cataracts and brakes
That humour interposed too often makes ;

All this still legible in memory's page,
And still to be so to my latest age,
Adds joy to duty, makes me glad to pay   70
Such honours to thee as my numbers may ;
Perhaps a frail memorial, but sincere,
Not scorned in heaven, though little noticed here.
   Could Time, his flight reversed, restore the hours,
When, playing with thy vesture's tissued flowers,   75
The violet, the pink, and jessamine,
I pricked them into paper with a pin
(And thou wast happier than myself the while,
Wouldst softly speak, and stroke my head and smile)—
Could those few pleasant days again appear,   80
Might one wish bring them, would I wish them here?
I would not trust my heart—the dear delight
Seems so to be desired, perhaps I might.
But no—what here we call our life is such
So little to be loved, and thou so much,   85
That I should ill requite thee to constrain
Thy unbound spirit into bonds again.
   Thou, as a gallant bark from Albion's coast
(The storms all weathered and the ocean crossed)
Shoots into port at some well-havened isle,   90
Where spices breathe, and brighter seasons smile,
There sits quiescent on the floods that show
Her beauteous form reflected clear below,
While airs impregnated with incense play
Around her, fanning light her streamers gay ;   95
So thou, with sails how swift ! hast reached the shore,
" Where tempests never beat nor billows roar,"
And thy loved consort on the dangerous tide
Of life long since has anchored by thy side.
But me, scarce hoping to attain that rest,   100
Always from port withheld, always distressed—
Me howling blasts drive devious, tempest-tost,
Sails ripped, seams opening wide, and compass lost,

And day by day some current's thwarting force
Sets me more distant from a prosperous course.   105
Yet, oh, the thought that thou art safe, and he !
That thought is joy, arrive what may to me.
My boast is not, that I deduce my birth
From loins enthroned and rulers of the earth ;
But higher far my proud pretentions rise—   110
The son of parents passed into the skies !
And now, farewell.—Time unrevoked has run
His wonted course, yet what I wished is done.
By contemplation's help, not sought in vain,
I seem to have lived my childhood o'er again ;   115
To have renewed the joys that once were mine,
Without the sin of violating thine :
And, while the wings of Fancy still are free,
And I can view this mimic show of thee,
Time has but half succeeded in his theft —   120
Thyself removed, thy power to soothe me left.

EPITAPH ON A HARE.

HERE lies, whom hound did ne'er pursue
    Nor swifter greyhound follow,
Whose foot ne'er tainted morning dew,
    Nor ear heard huntsman's halloo ;

Old Tiney, surliest of his kind,   5
    Who, nursed with tender care,
And to domestic bounds confined,   .
    Was still a wild Jack hare.

Though duly from my hand he took
    His pittance every night,   10
He did it with a jealous look,
    And, when he could, would bite.

His diet was of wheaten bread,
 And milk, and oats, and straw,
Thistles, or lettuces instead,   15
 With sand to scour his maw.

On twigs of hawthorn he regaled,
 On pippins' russet peel,
And, when his juicy salads failed,
 Sliced carrot pleased him well.   20

A Turkey carpet was his lawn,
 Whereon he loved to bound,
To skip and gambol like a fawn,
 And swing his rump around.

His frisking was at evening hours,   25
 For then he lost his fear,
But most before approaching showers,
 Or when a storm drew near.

Eight years and five round-rolling moons
 He thus saw steal away,   30
Dozing out all his idle noons,
 And every night at play.

I kept him for his humour's sake,
 For he would oft beguile
My heart of thoughts that made it ache, 35
 And force me to a smile.

But now beneath this walnut shade
 He finds his long last home,
And waits, in snug concealment laid,
 Till gentler Puss shall come.   40

He, still more agèd, feels the shocks
 From which no care can save,
And, partner once of Tiney's box,
 Must soon partake his grave.

⌐ON THE LOSS OF THE ROYAL GEORGE.

WRITTEN WHEN THE NEWS ARRIVED.

To the March in "Scipio."

TOLL for the brave !
   The brave that are no more !
All sunk beneath the wave,
   Fast by their native shore !

Eight hundred of the brave,   5
   Whose courage well was tried,
Had made the vessel heel,
   And laid her on her side.

A land-breeze shook the shrouds,
   And she was overset ;   10
Down went the Royal George,
   With all her crew complete.

Toll for the brave !
   Brave Kempenfelt is gone ;
His last sea-fight is fought ;   15
   His work of glory done.

It was not in the battle ;
   No tempest gave the shock ;
She sprang no fatal leak ;
   She ran upon no rock.   20

His sword was in its sheath ;
   His fingers held the pen,
When Kempenfelt went down
   With twice four hundred men.

Weigh the vessel up,   25
   Once dreaded by our foes !
And mingle with our cup
   The tears that England owes.

Her timbers yet are sound,
  And she may float again   30
Full charged with England's thunder,
  And plough the distant main.

But Kempenfelt is gone,
  His victories are o'er ;
And he and his eight hundred   35
  Shall plough the wave no more.

ON THE SHORTNESS OF HUMAN LIFE.

Suns that set, and moons that wane,
Rise and are restored again ;
Stars that orient day subdues
Night at her return renews.
Herbs and flowers, the beauteous birth   5
Of the genial womb of earth,
Suffer but a transient death
From the winter's cruel breath.
Zephyr speaks ; serener skies
Warm the glebe, and they arise.   10
We, alas ! earth's haughty kings,
We, that promise mighty things,
Losing soon life's happy prime,
Droop, and fade, in little time.
Spring returns, but not our bloom ;   15
Still 'tis winter in the tomb.

THE VALEDICTION.

Farewell, false hearts ! whose best affections fail,
Like shallow brooks which summer suns exhale !

Forgetful of the man whom once ye chose,
Cold in his cause, and careless of his woes,
I bid you both a long and last adieu, 5
Cold in my turn, and unconcerned like you.
　First, farewell Niger ! whom, now duly proved,
I disregard as much as once I loved.
Your brain well furnished, and your tongue well taught
To press with energy your ardent thought, 10
Your senatorial dignity of face,
Sound sense, intrepid spirit, manly grace,
Have raised you high as talents can ascend,
Made you a peer, but spoilt you for a friend !
Pretend to all that parts have e'er acquired ; 15
Be great, be feared, be envied, be admired ;
To fame as lasting as the earth pretend,
But not, hereafter, to the name of friend !
I sent you verse, and, as your lordship knows,
Backed with a modest sheet of humble prose ; 20
Not to recall a promise to your mind,
Fulfilled with ease had you been so inclined,
But to comply with feelings, and to give
Proof of an old affection still alive.
Your sullen silence serves at least to tell 25
Your altered heart ; and so, my lord, farewell !
　Next, busy actor on a meaner stage,
Amusement-monger of a trifling age,
Illustrious histrionic patentee,
Terentius, once my friend, farewell to thee ! 30
In thee some virtuous qualities combine
To fit thee for a nobler part than thine,
Who, born a gentleman, hast stooped too low,
To live by buskin, sock, and raree-show.
Thy schoolfellow, and partner of thy plays, 35
Where Nichol swung the birch and twined the bays,
And having known thee bearded, and full grown,
The weekly censor of a laughing town,

F

I thought the volume I presumed to send,
Graced with the name of a long-absent friend,   40
Might prove a welcome gift, and touch thine heart,
Not hard by nature, in a feeling part.
But thou, it seems, (what cannot grandeur do,
Though but a dream!) art grown disdainful too;
And strutting in thy school of queens and kings,   45
Who fret their hour and are forgotten things,
Hast caught the cold distemper of the day,
And, like his lordship, cast thy friend away.
    Oh, Friendship! cordial of the human breast!
So little felt, so fervently professed!   50
Thy blossoms deck our unsuspecting years;
The promise of delicious fruit appears:
We hug the hopes of constancy and truth,
Such is the folly of our dreaming youth;
But soon, alas! detect the rash mistake   55
That sanguine inexperience loves to make;
And view with tears the expected harvest lost,
Decayed by time, or withered by a frost.
Whoever undertakes a friend's great part
Should be renewed in nature, pure in heart,   60
Prepared for martyrdom, and strong to prove
A thousand ways the force of genuine love.
He may be called to give up health and gain,
To exchange content for trouble, ease for pain,
To echo sigh for sigh, and groan for groan,   65
And wet his cheeks with sorrows not his own.
The heart of man, for such a task too frail,
When most relied on is most sure to fail;
And, summoned to partake its fellow's woe,
Starts from its office like a broken bow.   70
    Votaries of business and of pleasure prove
Faithless alike in friendship and in love.
Retired from all the circles of the gay,
And all the crowds that bustle life away,

To scenes where competition, envy, strife,   75
Beget no thunder-clouds to trouble life,
Let me, the charge of some good angel, find
One who has known and has escaped mankind ;
Polite, yet virtuous, who has brought away
The manners, not the morals, of the day :   80
With him, perhaps with *her* (for men have known
No firmer friendship than the fair have shown)
Let me enjoy, in some unthought-of spot,
All former friends forgiven and forgot,
Down to the close of life's fast-fading scene,   85
Union of hearts, without a flaw between.
'Tis grace, 'tis bounty, and it calls for praise,
If God give health, that sunshine of our days !
And if He add, a blessing shared by few,
Content of heart, more praises still are due :   90
But if He grant a friend, that boon possessed
Indeed is treasure, and crowns all the rest ;
And giving one, whose heart is in the skies,
Born from above, and made divinely wise,
He gives, what bankrupt Nature never can,   95
Whose noblest coin is light and brittle man,
Gold, purer far than Ophir ever knew,
A soul, an image of Himself, and therefore true.

GRATITUDE.

ADDRESSED TO LADY HESKETH.

This cap, that so stately appears,
   With ribbon-bound tassel on high,
Which seems by the crest that it rears
   Ambitious of brushing the sky :
This cap to my cousin I owe,   5
   She gave it, and gave me beside,

Wreathed into an elegant bow,
    The ribbon with which it is tied.

This wheel-footed studying chair,
    Contrived both for toil and repose,   10
Wide-elbowed, and wadded with hair,
    In which I both scribble and doze,
Bright-studded to dazzle the eyes,
    And rival in lustre of that
In which, or astronomy lies,   15
    Fair Cassiopeïa sat :

These carpets, so soft to the foot,
    Caledonia's traffic and pride !
Oh spare them, ye knights of the boot,
    Escaped from a cross-country ride !   20
This table and mirror within,
    Secure from collision and dust,
At which I oft shave cheek and chin,
    And periwig nicely adjust:

This movable structure of shelves,   25
    For its beauty admired and its use,
And charged with octavos and twelves,
    The gayest I had to produce ;
Where, flaming in scarlet and gold,
    My poems enchanted I view,   30
And hope, in due time, to behold
    My Iliad and Odyssey too :

This china, that decks the alcove,
    Which here people call a buffet,
But what the gods call it above   35
    Has ne'er been revealed to us yet :
These curtains, that keep the room warm
    ɾ Or cool, as the season demands :
These stoves, that for pattern and form
    Seem the labour of Mulciber's hands :   40

All these are not half that I owe
   To one, from our earliest youth
To me ever ready to show
   Benignity, friendship, and truth ;
For Time, the destroyer declared   45
   And foe of our perishing kind,
If even her face he has spared,
   Much less could he alter her mind.

Thus compassed about with the goods
   And chattels of leisure and ease,   50
I indulge my poetical moods
   In many such fancies as these ;
And fancies I fear they will seem —
   Poets' goods are not often so fine ;
The poets will swear that I dream   55
   When I sing of the splendour of mine.

THE MORNING DREAM.

'Twas in the glad season of spring,
   Asleep at the dawn of the day,
I dreamed what I cannot but sing,
   So pleasant it seemed as I lay.
I dreamed that, on ocean afloat,   5
   Far hence to the westward I sailed,
While the billows high-lifted the boat,
   And the fresh-blowing breeze never failed.

In the steerage a woman I saw ;
   Such at least was the form that she wore,   10
Whose beauty impressed me with awe,
   Never taught me by woman before.
She sat, and a shield at her side
   Shed light like a sun on the waves,

And smiling divinely, she cried :   15
  "I go to make freemen of slaves."

Then raising her voice to a strain
  The sweetest that ear ever heard,
She sang of the slave's broken chain
  Wherever her glory appeared.   20
Some clouds, which had over us hung,
  Fled, chased by her melody clear,
And methought while she liberty sung,
  'Twas liberty only to hear.

Thus swiftly dividing the flood,   25
  To a slave-cultured island we came,
Where a Demon, her enemy, stood—
  Oppression his terrible name.
In his hand, as the sign of his sway,
  A scourge hung with lashes he bore,   30
And stood looking out for his prey
  From Africa's sorrowful shore.

But soon as, approaching the land,
  That goddess-like woman he viewed,
The scourge he let fall from his hand,   35
  With blood of his subjects imbrued.
I saw him both sicken and die,
  And, the moment the monster expired,
Heard shouts that ascended the sky,
  From thousands with rapture inspired.   40

Awaking, how could I but muse
  At what such a dream should betide ?
But soon my ear caught the glad news,
  Which served my weak thought for a guide,—
That Britannia, renowned o'er the waves   45
  For the hatred she ever has shown
To the black-sceptred rulers of slaves,
  Resolves to have none of her own.

THE RETIRED CAT.

A POET's cat, sedate and grave
As poet well could wish to have,
Was much addicted to inquire
For nooks to which she might retire,
And where, secure as mouse in chink,   5
She might repose, or sit and think.
I know not where she caught the trick,—
Nature perhaps herself had cast her
In such a mould philosophique,
Or else she learned it of her master.   10
Sometimes ascending, debonair,
An apple-tree, or lofty pear,
Lodged with convenience in the fork,
She watched the gardener at his work ;
Sometimes her ease and solace sought   15
In an old empty watering-pot ;
There, wanting nothing save a fan
To seem some nymph in her sedan,
Apparelled in exactest sort,
And ready to be borne to court.   20
    But love of change, it seems, has place
Not only in our wiser race ;
Cats also feel, as well as we,
That passion's force, and so did she.
Her climbing, she began to find,   25
Exposed her too much to the wind,
And the old utensil of tin
Was cold and comfortless within :
She therefore wished instead of those
Some place of more serene repose,   30
Where neither cold might come, nor air
Too rudely wanton with her hair,
And sought it in the likeliest mode
Within her master's snug abode.

A drawer, it chanced, at bottom lined   35
With linen of the softest kind,
With such as merchants introduce
From India, for the ladies' use—
A drawer impending o'er the rest,
Half open in the topmost chest,   40
Of depth enough, and none to spare,
Invited her to slumber there ;
Puss with delight beyond expression
Surveyed the scene, and took possession.
Recumbent at her ease ere long,   45
And lulled by her own humdrum song,
She left the cares of life behind,
And slept as she would sleep her last,
When in came, housewifely inclined,
The chambermaid, and shut it fast ;   50
By no malignity impelled,
But all unconscious whom it held.
    Awakened by the shock, cried Puss,
" Was ever cat attended thus !
The open drawer was left, I see,   55
Merely to prove a nest for me.
For soon as I was well composed,
Then came the maid, and it was closed.
How smooth these 'kerchiefs, and how sweet !
Oh, what a delicate retreat !   60
I will resign myself to rest
Till Sol, declining in the west,
Shall call to supper, when, no doubt,
Susan will come and let me out."
    The evening came, the sun descended,   65
And puss remained still unattended.
The night rolled tardily away
(With her indeed 'twas never day),
The sprightly morn her course renewed,
The evening gray again ensued,   70

And puss came into mind no more
Than if entombed the day before.
With hunger pinched, and pinched for room,
She now presaged approaching doom,
Nor slept a single wink, or purred,   75
Conscious of jeopardy incurred.
    That night, by chance, the poet watching,
Heard an inexplicable scratching ;
His noble heart went pit-a-pat,
And to himself he said—" What's that ? "   80
He drew the curtain at his side,
And forth he peeped, but nothing spied ;
Yet, by his ear directed, guessed
Something imprisoned in the chest,
And, doubtful what, with prudent care   85
Resolved it should continue there.
At length, a voice which well he knew,
A long and melancholy mew,
Saluting his poetic ears,
Consoled him, and dispelled his fears ;   90
He left his bed, he trod the floor,
He 'gan in haste the drawers explore,
The lowest first, and without stop
The rest in order to the top ;
For 'tis a truth well known to most,   95
That whatsoever thing is lost,
We seek it, ere it come to light,
In every cranny but the right.
Forth skipped the cat, not now replete
As erst with airy self-conceit,   100
Nor in her own fond apprehension
A theme for all the world's attention,
But modest, sober, cured of all
Her notions hyperbolical,
And wishing for a place of rest   105
Anything rather than a chest.

Then stept the poet into bed,
With this reflection in his head :

MORAL.

Beware of too sublime a sense
Of your own worth and consequence.   110
The man who dreams himself so great,
And his importance of such weight,
That all around in all that's done
Must move and act for him alone,
Will learn in school of tribulation   115
The folly of his expectation.

EPITAPH ON "FOP,"

A DOG BELONGING TO LADY THROCKMORTON.

THOUGH once a puppy, and though Fop by name,
Here moulders one whose bones some honour claim ;
No sycophant, although of spaniel race,
And though no hound, a martyr to the chase.
Ye squirrels, rabbits, leverets, rejoice !   5
Your haunts no longer echo to his voice ;
This record of his fate exulting view,
He died worn out with vain pursuit of you.
    "Yes"—the indignant shade of Fop replies—
"And worn with vain pursuit man also dies."   10

TO MRS. UNWIN.

MARY ! I want a lyre with other strings,
Such aid from Heaven as some have feigned they drew,
An eloquence scarce given to mortals, new
And undebased by praise of meaner things,

That, ere through age or woe I shed my wings,   5
I may record thy worth with honour due,
In verse as musical as thou art true,
And that immortalizes whom it sings.
But thou hast little need.   There is a book
By seraphs writ with beams of heavenly light,   10
On which the eyes of God not rarely look,
A chronicle of actions just and bright :
There all thy deeds, my faithful Mary, shine,
And, since thou own'st that praise, I spare thee mine.

TO MARY.

THE twentieth year is well-nigh past,
Since first our sky was overcast ;
Ah, would that this might be the last !
    My Mary !

Thy spirits have a fainter flow,   5
I see thee daily weaker grow ;
'Twas my distress that brought thee low,
    My Mary !

Thy needles, once a shining store,
For my sake restless heretofore,   10
Now rust disused, and shine no more,
    My Mary !

For though thou gladly wouldst fulfil
The same kind office for me still,
Thy sight now seconds not thy will,   15
    My Mary !

But well thou playedst the housewife's part,
And all thy threads with magic art
Have wound themselves about this heart,
    My Mary !   20

Thy indistinct expressions seem
Like language uttered in a dream ;
Yet me they charm, whate'er the theme,
                    My Mary !

Thy silver locks, once auburn bright,   25
Are still more lovely in my sight,
Than golden beams of orient light,
                    My Mary !

For, could I view nor them nor thee,
What sight worth seeing could I see ?   30
The sun would rise in vain for me,
                    My Mary !

Partakers of thy sad decline,
Thy hands their little force resign ;
Yet, gently pressed, press gently mine,   35
                    My Mary !

Such feebleness of limbs thou provest,
That now at every step thou movest
Upheld by two, yet still thou lovest,
                    My Mary !   40

And still to love, though pressed with ill,
In wintry age to feel no chill,
With me is to be lovely still, ·
                    My Mary !

But ah ! by constant heed I know,   45
How oft the sadness that I show
Transforms thy smiles to looks of woe,
                    My Mary !

And should my future lot be cast
With much resemblance of the past,   50
Thy worn-out heart will break at last,
                    My Mary !

THE CASTAWAY.

Obscurest night involved the sky,
    The Atlantic billows roared,
When such a destined wretch as I,
    Washed headlong from on board,
Of friends, of hope, of all bereft,   5
His floating home for ever left.

No braver chief could Albion boast
    Than he with whom he went,
Nor ever ship left Albion's coast
    With warmer wishes sent.   10
He loved them both, but both in vain,
Nor him beheld, nor her again.

Not long beneath the whelming brine,
    Expert to swim, he lay ;
Nor soon he felt his strength decline,   15
    Or courage die away ;
But waged with death a lasting strife,
Supported by despair of life.

He shouted : nor his friends had failed
    To check the vessel's course,   20
But so the furious blast prevailed,
    That, pitiless perforce,
They left their outcast mate behind,
And scudded still before the wind.

Some succour yet they could afford ;   25
    And such as storms allow,
The cask, the coop, the floated cord,
    Delayed not to bestow.
But he, they knew, nor ship nor shore,
Whate'er they gave, should visit more.   30

Nor, cruel as it seemed, could he
    Their haste himself condemn,

Aware that flight, in such a sea,
   Alone could rescue them ;
Yet bitter felt it still to die   35
Deserted, and his friends so nigh.

He long survives, who lives an hour
   In ocean, self-upheld ;
And so long he, with unspent power,
   His destiny repelled ;   40
And ever, as the minutes flew,
Entreated help, or cried " Adieu ! "

At length, his transient respite past,
   His comrades, who before
Had heard his voice in every blast,   45
   Could catch the sound no more :
For then, by toil subdued, he drank
The stifling wave, and then he sank.

No poet wept him ; but the page
   Of narrative sincere,   50
That tells his name, his worth, his age,
   Is wet with Anson's tear :
And tears by bards or heroes shed
Alike immortalize the dead.

I therefore purpose not, or dream,   55
   Descanting on his fate,
To give the melancholy theme
   A more enduring date :
But misery still delights to trace
Its semblance in another's case.   60

No voice divine the storm allayed,
   No light propitious shone,
When, snatched from all effectual aid,
   We perished, each alone :
But I beneath a rougher sea,   65
And whelmed in deeper gulfs than he.

STRADA'S NIGHTINGALE.

THE shepherd touched his reed ; sweet Philomel
  Essayed, and oft essayed to catch the strain,
And treasuring, as on her ear they fell,
  The numbers, echoed note for note again.

The peevish youth, who ne'er had found before   5
  A rival of his skill, indignant heard,
And soon (for various was his tuneful store)
  In loftier tones defied the simple bird.

She dared the task, and rising as he rose,
  With all the force that passion gives inspired,   10
Returned the sounds awhile, but in the close,
  Exhausted fell, and at his feet expired.

Thus strength, not skill, prevailed.   O fatal strife,
  By thee, poor songstress, playfully begun !
And oh, sad victory, which cost thy life,   15
  And he may wish that he had never won.

THE COLUBRIAD.

CLOSE by the threshold of a door nailed fast
Three kittens sat ; each kitten looked aghast.
I, passing swift and inattentive by,
At the three kittens cast a careless eye ;
Not much concerned to know what they did there,   5
Not deeming kittens worth a poet's care.
But presently a loud and furious hiss
Caused me to stop, and to exclaim, " What's this ?"
When lo ! upon the threshold met my view,
With head erect, and eyes of fiery hue,   10
A viper, long as Count de Grasse's queue.

Forth from his head his forkèd tongue he throws,
Darting it full against a kitten's nose ;
Who having never seen, in field or house,
The like, sat still and silent as a mouse ;   15
Only projecting, with attention due,
Her whiskered face, she asked him, " Who are you ?"
On to the hall went I, with pace not slow,
But swift as lightning, for a long Dutch hoe :
With which well armed I hastened to the spot,   20
To find the viper, but I found him not.
And turning up the leaves and shrubs around,
Found only that he was not to be found.
But still the kittens, sitting as before,
Sat watching close the bottom of the door.   25
" I hope," said I, " the villain I would kill
Has slipped between the door and the door-sill ;
And if I make despatch, and follow hard,
No doubt but I shall find him in the yard :"
For long ere now it should have been rehearsed,   30
'Twas in the garden that I found him first.
E'en there I found him, there the full-grown cat
His head, with velvet paw, did gently pat ;
As curious as the kittens erst had been
To learn what this phenomenon might mean.   35
Filled with heroic ardour at the sight,
And fearing every moment he would bite,
And rob our household of our only cat
That was of age to combat with a rat,
With outstretched hoe I slew him at the door,   40
And taught him NEVER TO COME THERE NO MORE.

ON A MISCHIEVOUS BULL,

WHICH THE OWNER OF HIM SOLD AT THE AUTHOR'S INSTANCE.

Go ! thou art all unfit to share
    The pleasures of this place
With such as its old tenants are,
    Creatures of gentler race.

The squirrel here his hoard provides,   5
    Aware of wintry storms,
And woodpeckers explore the sides
    Of rugged oaks for worms.

The sheep here smooths the knotted thorn
    With frictions of her fleece ;   10
And here I wander eve and morn,
    Like her, a friend to peace.

Ah ! I could pity thee exiled
    From this secure retreat—
I would not lose it to be styled   15
    The happiest of the great.

But thou canst taste no calm delight ;
    Thy pleasure is to show
Thy magnanimity in fight,
    Thy prowess ; therefore go !   20

I care not whether east or north,
    So I no more may find thee ;
The angry Muse thus sings thee forth,
    And claps the gate behind thee.

NOTES.

A FABLE.

INTRODUCTION.

This poem was first published in *Poems*, 1782. It was written on May 9, 1780, as we find from a letter of the poet's to Newton (who had removed from Olney Vicarage to London on the preceding January), May 10, 1780, in which he says: "A crow, rook, or raven, has built a nest in one of the young elm trees at the side of Mrs. Aspray's orchard.[1] In a violent storm that blew yesterday morning, I saw it agitated to a degree that seemed to threaten its immediate destruction, and versified the following thoughts upon the occasion."

NOTES.

3. **her wicker-work**, *i.e.* her nest, made of twigs interlaced.

4. **Her chickens**, etc. In allusion to the proverb, "Do not count your chickens before they are hatched," *i.e.* do not be over-confident of future advantage.

8, 9. **'Twas April … May.** In 1582 Pope Gregory XIII., in order to rectify the errors of the current calendar, published a new one, in which ten days were omitted. The new style was not adopted by Great Britain till 1752, in which year eleven days were left out of the calendar, the 3rd September being reckoned as the 14th September. For many years afterwards the old reckoning was jealously adhered to by the rural population. Stanhope (*Hist. of England*, iii. 508) tells us that in 1754 Lord Macclesfield's eldest son was assailed at a contested election

---

[1] This orchard lay between Cowper's garden and the vicarage garden, and gave the name to his house, 'Orchard Side.'

62

in Oxfordshire with vehement cries of "Give us back our eleven days!"

15. **her golden hopes,** her treasured eggs, which were so full of promise.

18. **Ralph,** a familiar name of the raven. Observe that the *l* is not sounded here, as in *calf, half,* etc.

20. **birds of omen.** Cf. Shaks. *Macbeth,* I. v. 36-38:

> " The raven himself is hoarse
> That croaks the fatal entrance of Duncan
> Under my battlements."

And Macaulay, *History of St. Kilda,* p. 174 : "Of inspired birds ravens were accounted the most prophetical. Accordingly, in the language of that district, ' to have the foresight of a raven ' is to this day a proverbial expression.'

24. **Hodge** is the name of a rustic, the " goodman" of Gammer Gurton in the old play of *Gammer Gurton's Needle,* written about 1564 by John Still. Hence the name is applied to any country fellow.

27. **A gift ... fair.** Cf. Shenstone's song :

> " I have found out a gift for my fair !
> I have found where the wood-pigeons breed ;
> But let me that plunder forbear ;
> She will say 'twas a barbarous deed."

For *fair* see note, p. 70, l. 26.

28. **dray** (or *drey*), a squirrel's nest. Cf. Drayton, *Quest of Cynthia* :

> " The nimble squirrel noting here,
> Her mossy *dray* that makes."

34. **bid,** bid by Providence, ordained.

35. **that's strangled by a hair.** Hyperbolically for ' who meets his death by some insignificant cause.'

A COMPARISON.

INTRODUCTION.

This short piece was first published in *Poems,* 1782. The comparison of human life to a river that is lost in the ocean of eternity is not uncommon in poetry. Cf. Hawkesworth's well-known verses beginning "Through groves sequestered, dark, and still."

NOTES.

4. can bribe, *i.e.* to stay.

6. ocean. Time is swallowed by the ocean of eternity. Cf. Denham, *Cooper's Hill* (of the Thames):

> "Hasting to pay his tribute to the sea,
> Like mortal life to meet eternity."

10. laughs, 'looks cheerful.' The metaphor is common in poetry; cf. Gray, *The Bard*, 71, "Fair laughs the Morn"; Ovid, *Metaph.* xv. 206, *Ridet ager*, 'The field laughs.'

11. the nobler mind, the mind which is nobler than or superior to "the land."

12. Neglected, *i.e.* through not being made a proper use of. If men fail to devote their time to the improvement of their minds, moral barrenness is the result.

ANOTHER.

INTRODUCTION.

This piece was first published in *Poems*, 1782. The "young lady" mentioned in the title is Miss Shuttleworth, Mrs. William Unwin's sister. Cowper enclosed the verses in a letter to Unwin, June 8th, 1780, with the heading, "An English Versification of a Thought that popped into my Head about two Months since," and wrote at their close: "Now this is not so exclusively applicable to a maiden as to be the sole property of your sister, Shuttleworth. If you look at Mrs. Unwin, you will see that she has not lost her right to this just praise by marrying you."

NOTES.

5. prevailing, 'irresistible.' Cf. Denham, *Cooper's Hill* (of the Thames):

> "Oh could I flow like thee! and make thy stream
> My great example, as it is my theme;
> Though deep yet clear, though gentle yet not dull;
> *Strong without rage*, without o'erflowing full."

9. that watery glass, the stream, which is as clear as glass.

10. And heaven reflected, for 'and with heaven reflected.' As the stream mirrors the sky, so heavenly or spiritual feelings shine in the looks of the "virtuous maid."

ALEXANDER SELKIRK.

INTRODUCTION.

These verses were first published in *Poems*, 1782. Alexander Selkirk was born in 1676, at the village of Largo, in Fifeshire. He ran away to sea in 1695, and some years later joined a buccaneering expedition under the famous Captain Dampier, when they put in at the desert island of Juan Fernandez for water. Dissension had raged among the crew of Selkirk's ship, who was so disgusted with the conduct of his captain, a quarrelsome and ferocious ruffian named Stradling, that he resolved to remain on the island. He was taken at his word, though he speedily repented of his determination, and left there with his gun, a hatchet, and a knife, and a few other useful articles that had been put ashore with him. With the help of these he managed to subsist, but he appears to have sunk to the condition of worse than a savage, for, when discovered, he had almost entirely lost the use of language, which he regained only after a considerable time. He remained alone on the island from September, 1704, to February, 1709, a period of over four years and four months, when, he was rescued by Captain Woodes Rogers, and returned to England in 1711. He went to sea again in 1717, and ultimately attained the rank of lieutenant in H.M.S. *Weymouth*, on board of which he died in 1723. In 1712 an account of him was published by Captain Rogers, and in the following year Sir Richard Steele repeated the tale of his adventures in *The Englishman*, December, 1713, which are said to have suggested to Daniel Defoe the groundwork of his celebrated story, *Robinson Crusoe*, published in 1719.

Juan Fernandez is a small island in the South Pacific Ocean, 450 miles west of the coast of Chili. A monument to Selkirk was placed on the island by the officers of H.M.S. *Challenger*, in 1874.

NOTES.

1, 3. Mr. Griffith has a long note on this so-called 'Irish rhyme'—the word *sea* rhyming with *survey*, and remarks that "the scrupulous Pope made *sea* rhyme with *they* (Sappho to Phaon, 222), and with *day* (Statius, I. 279). Again, he gives *tea* as a rhyme to *away* (Rape of the Lock, I. 62), to *obey* (ib. III. 7) and to *stay* (The Basset-Table, 28)." Now we know that the old pronunciation of *tea* was *tay*, so that it would seem that other words in which the letters *ea* are found together were also so pronounced; cf. note, p. 103, ll. 41, 42. A similar rhyme occurs in *The Dog and the Water-Lily*, 41, 43, where *enjoin* (pronounced *enjine*) is made to rhyme with *thine*.

2. **none** is singular here (= no one). When applied to persons
it is now plural in meaning, with singular 'no one.'

3. **From the centre ... sea,** *i.e.* over the whole extent of the
island.

4. **the fowl and the brute,** all birds and beasts. *The* here
indicates a specimen as representative of a class.

5. **O Solitude!** etc. An instance of the figure Apostrophe;
cf. ll. 17, 25, 33. The question is a rhetorical one, equivalent to
'I cannot find the charms,' etc.

6. **sages.** Bacon (Essay on Friendship) quotes from Aristotle,
"Whosoever is delighted in solitude is either a wild beast or a
god." He mentions as instances of men who have sought solitude for a good purpose, "divers of the ancient hermits and holy
fathers of the Church."

7. **Better dwell,** elliptical for 'It is better to dwell.'

9. **humanity's,** mankind's—abstract for concrete.

10. **my journey,** *i.e.* the journey of life; my life; Cf. *Receipt
of my Mother's Picture,* 24.

12. **I start at,** etc. Selkirk, having no one to speak to,
naturally seldom spoke, so that the sound of his own voice grew
strange and almost alarming to him.   See Introduction.

15, 16. **They are so ... shocking to me.** They show no fear of
me, having never been hunted; and since their tameness arises
from their never having had anything to do with man, it is not
pleasing but painful to me, because it adds to my feeling of
loneliness.   Cf. Tennyson, *Enoch Arden,* 552, 553 (of animal life
in the lonely island):

" Nor save for pity was it hard to take
    The helpless life so wild that it was tame."

And Darwin, *Variations of Animals and Plants under Domestica-
tion,* pp. 20, 21: "Quadrupeds and birds which have seldom
been disturbed by man dread him no more than do our English
birds the cows or horses grazing in the fields."

18. **Divinely,** by God.

19. **had I,** if I had. Cf. note, p. 71, l. 15; and Bible, *Psalms,*
lv. 6: "And I (David) said, Oh that I had wings like a dove!
for then would I fly away and be at rest."

22. **In the ways of,** by the pursuit or cultivation of.

24. **sallies,** merry outbursts, mirthful sayings; Lat. *salire,* 'to
leap.'

25. **untold,** uncounted, incalculable. A frequent meaning of
tell in earlier English was 'count,' and similarly *tale* meant a
number, a reckoning. Milton, enumerating the various rural
occupations of the early morning in *L'Allegro,* 63-68, says that

"Every shepherd *tells* his *tale*," *i.e.* counts his sheep. Those who count the votes at a division in the House of Commons are still called the ' tellers.'

27. **than silver and gold.** So Solomon (*Proverbs*, viii. 10) makes Divine Wisdom say: "Receive my instruction and not silver ; and knowledge rather than choice gold."

29. **the church-going bell,** the bell that belongs to or accompanies the going to church. *Going* is not a participle, but a verbal noun.

31, 32. **sighed ... smiled.** Human feelings of sadness and of joy are attributed to the valleys and rocks, because the scenes of nature are coloured by our feelings. Hence *sighed* means 'had a sad aspect,' and *smiled* means 'had a joyful aspect.' *Knell* is the tolling of the church bell at a death or funeral.

32. **sabbath,** the Day of Rest, Sunday ; *Sabbath* being Hebrew for ' rest.' It is said that Selkirk was careful, while on the island, to measure the lapse of time and distinguish Sunday from the other days of the week.

37-40. He yearns, in his loneliness, for human friendship, and feels as if his friends must have all forgotten him. In his despair, it is something to know that he has a friend still, though he will never see him. Cf. Tennyson, *Enoch Arden*, 576-578 :

> "What he fain had seen
> He could not see, the kindly human face,
> Nor ever hear a kindly voice."

44. **light** travels at the rate of nearly 200,000 miles in a second of time.

45-48. With the simplicity of statement and sentiment here it is interesting to compare the nineteenth-century elaboration of a similar feeling in *Enoch Arden*, 596-617 :

> " There often as he watch'd or seem'd to watch,
>
> .   .   .   .
>
> So still, the golden lizard on him paused,
> A phantom made of many phantoms moved
> Before him haunting him, or he himself
> Moved haunting people, things and places, known
> Far in a darker isle beyond the line ;
> The babes, their babble, Annie, the small house,
> The climbing street, the mill, the leafy lanes,
>
> .   .   .   .
>
> Once likewise, in the ringing of his ears,
> Tho' faintly, merrily—far and far away—
> He heard the pealing of his parish bells ;
> Then, tho' he knew not wherefore, started up
> Shuddering, and when the beauteous hateful isle

Return'd upon him, had not his poor heart
Spoken with That, which being everywhere
Lets none, who speaks with Him, seem all alone,
Surely the man had died of solitude."

50. lair, lit. a couching-place, is from the same root as *lie*.

52. repair, resort, go. Cf. note, p. 89, l. 10. Skeat and Brachet derive the word from Lat. *repatriare*, 'to return to one's country'; Wedgwood from Ital. *riparo*, 'a shelter,' from *riparare*, 'to defend.'

55. Gives ... a grace, *i.e.* softens or relieves it.

REPORT OF AN ADJUDGED CASE.

INTRODUCTION.

These witty verses were first published in *Poems*, 1782. Enclosing them in a letter to Joseph Hill, December 25, 1780, Cowper writes : " Happy is the man who knows just so much of the law as to make himself a little merry now and then with the solemnity of judicial proceedings. I have heard of common law judgments before now, indeed, I have been present at the delivery of some, that, according to my poor apprehension, while they paid the utmost respect to the letter of a statute, have departed widely from the spirit of it ; and, being governed entirely by the point of law, have left equity, reason, and common sense behind them at an infinite distance. You will judge whether the following report of a case, drawn up by myself, be not a proof and illustration of this satirical assertion." In a subsequent letter to Hill, February 15, 1781, he says : " I am glad you were pleased with my report of so extraordinary a case. If the thought of versifying the decisions of our courts of justice had struck me, while I had the honour to attend them, it would perhaps have been no difficult matter to have compiled a volume of such amusing and interesting precedents." He sent the lines also to Unwin with a playful letter, dated December, 1780, in which he wittily advocates the desirability of poetical reports of law cases. The title of the MS. of this poem in the British Museum runs thus :

Nose Plf. ; Eyes Deft. ;
Vid. Plowden, folio 6,000.

i.e. " Nose Plaintiff; Eyes Defendants "; the reference to Plowden (an eminent lawyer, author of Law Commentaries) being, of course, a playful one.

NOTES.

8. nicely, exactly, accurately. Cf. note, p. 103, l. 63

11. had ... in wear, had in wearing, worn.

12. **time out of mind,** from time immemorial ; through all time. *Time* is to be parsed as in the adverbial objective case.

14. **straddle.** The verb *straddle* is for *striddle*, the frequentative form of *stride*.

17. **would your lordship,** if your lordship would. Cf. notes, p. 71, l. 15 ; p. 110, l. 34. '

19. **visage or countenance.** The repetition is in accordance with legal phraseology.

30. **without one if or but,** without any reservation ; unconditionally, absolutely. *If* and *but* are nouns here.

THE LILY AND THE ROSE.

INTRODUCTION.

This piece was first published in *Poems,* 1782, together with a Latin version of it, by the same author. It was included in a letter to Unwin, in which Cowper says : "As I promised you verse, if you would send me a frank, I am not willing to return the cover without some, though I think I have already wearied you by the prolixity of my prose." The letter is undated, but is assigned by Southey to the autumn of 1786.

NOTES.

1. **The nymph.** See note, p. 96, l. 1.

11. **a poet's page.** Cf. Shakspere's *Bridal Song*:

> " Roses, their sharp spines being gone,
> Not *royal* in their smells alone,
> But in their hue."

Also, Waller's " Go, lovely Rose " ; William Browne's *The Rose* ; Herrick's *The Funeral Rites of the Rose.*

13. **bespoke command,** was expressive of sovereignty.

15. **Flora's.** She was goddess of flowers (see l. 18, below) among the Romans.

17. **civil bickering,** intestine strife ; *civil* is used as in 'civil war.' *Bicker,* to skirmish, is the frequentative form of *pick,* in its original sense of to peck with the *beak.*

20. **the parterre,** the garden-plots. The French *parterre,* a garden laid out in beds, is from Lat. *per terram,* 'along the ground,' in allusion to the ground being made smooth and even.

21. She, of course, addresses the rose in this line, and the lily in the next.

26. **fair**, fair one, fair lady ; cf. *John Gilpin*, 5, "her *dear*," and note. 'The fair' for 'lady' or 'ladies' is common in poetry ; cf. note, p. 63, l. 27 ; and *Task*, iv. 53, 54 :

> " Silence, which the *fair*,
> Though eloquent themselves, yet fear to break."

27. **her cheeks**, alluding to the mingled white and red in her complexion. Cf. Campion's song :

> " There is a garden in her face,
> Where roses and white lilies blow."

And Cowper's letter to Unwin, May 3, 1784 (on rouging) : " Her roses and lilies were never discovered to be spurious, till she attained an age that made the supposition of their being natural impossible."

THE NIGHTINGALE AND THE GLOW-WORM.

INTRODUCTION.

This fable in verse was first published in *Poems*, 1782. In a letter to Unwin, February 27, 1780, Cowper says : " My whisking wit has produced the following (viz. this poem), the subject of which is more important than the manner in which I have treated it seems to imply, but a fable may speak truth, and all truth is sterling ; I only premise, that in the philosophical tract in the Register, I found it asserted that the glow-worm is the nightingale's proper food." The poet means that, while the manner or style of the poem is light and unpretending, its subject or moral is important.

NOTES.

1. **nightingale** (O.E. *nightegale*, from *nihte*, 'of night,' and *gale*, 'singer,' from *galan*, 'to sing,' means lit. 'singer of the night,' the bird that sings by night.

all day long. *Day* is to be parsed as an adverbial objective of time, modifying the adverb *long*.   Cf. note, p. 77, l. 22.

2. **his song**. Cowper correctly makes his nightingale masculine here. It is the male bird that is the singer, though the poets almost universally make it female, *philomela* being a feminine noun in Latin. In *Strada's Nightingale* (see ll. 3, 9), the bird is *she*.

3. **suspended**, stopt for the time.

9. A something. The use of the article before *something* shows that it has become a single word; we could not say 'a some book.'

10. glow-worm is for *glowing-worm*, like *spring-tide* for *springing-tide*, *screech-owl* for *screeching-owl*, etc.

11. stooping is a term applied to the swooping down, on the wing, of a bird of prey.

12. put him in his crop, swallow him. The *crop* is a receptacle at the bottom of a bird's throat, into which the food passes before it goes on into the stomach. Its sides are very elastic, and it is capable of containing a large quantity of food.

13. The worm. The glow-worm is not a worm at all, but an insect of the Coleoptera or beetle order. It is about half an inch in length; the males are winged, but the females are quite wingless, and so can only crawl. Both sexes have the power of emitting a phosphorescent light like that of the firefly; that emitted by the male is very faint, but the female gives a brilliant light, and is said to emit it to attract the male.

15. Did you admire, *i.e.* if you admired; cf. note, p. 69, l. 17.

19. self-same. The M.E. *self* was used in the sense of 'same' or 'very,' so that *self-same* is a cumulative word; cf. note, p. 115, l. 2.

22. beautify and cheer. 'Beautify' is to be taken with 'light,' and 'cheer' with 'music.'

23. songster. The suffix *-ster* was originally a feminine suffix, as in *spinster*. Hence in *songstress*, *i.e.* *songster-ess*, (as in *sempstress*) we have the French feminine suffix *-ess* needlessly affixed. Cowper uses *songstress* in *Strada's Nightingale*, 14.

27. Hence, from this fable.

jarring sectaries, quarrelsome members of religious sects; people who are always disputing with one another on religious points of difference.

30. worry and devour. Cf. St. Paul's exhortation to the Galatian Christians (*Gal.* v. 14, 15): "Thou shalt love thy neighbour as thyself. But if ye bite and devour one another, take heed that ye be not consumed one of another."

31. by sweet consent, by amicable agreement. They should "agree to differ."

33, 34. Respecting ... grace, treating with consideration the special qualities that others may possess (though differing from their own)—qualities which are bestowed by Nature or by God's Spirit.

37. the duty and the prize. To aim at peace is both a duty and a privilege. Peace is itself a reward to those who attain it.

38. **him that creeps and him that flies**, of everybody, high and low alike. The phrase, of course, takes us back to the glow-worm and nightingale of the fable. Here we have another reminiscence of Gray (see note, p. 80, l. 34), *Ode on Spring*, 33, 34:

"And they that creep and they that fly
Shall end where they began."

Cf. also Pope, *Essay on Man*, i. 12:

"All who blindly creep or sightless soar."

ON A GOLDFINCH.

INTRODUCTION.

This poem was first published in *Poems*, 1782. In a letter enclosing the piece to Unwin, November 9, 1780, Cowper writes: "I wrote the following last summer. The tragical occasion of it really happened in the next house to ours. I am glad when I can find a subject to work upon; a lapidary, I suppose, accounts it a laborious part of his business to rub away the roughness of the stone; but it is my amusement, and if after all the polishing I can give it, it discovers some little lustre, I think myself well rewarded for my pains."

NOTES.

2, 3. These two lines form two absolute clauses with 'being' understood. Similarly ll. 5 and 6 form three more such clauses.

5. **genteel**, 'graceful,' is a doublet of *gentle* and *gentile*, and means lit. 'of noble family,' from Lat. *gens, gentis*, a tribe or race. The word has become vulgarised in modern English, with the sense of 'well-bred, stylish.'

7. **But gaudy plumage**, etc. The classical examples of this repetition of previous expressions are Shaks. *As You Like It*, II. vii. 112-123, and Milton, *Par. Lost*, iv. 641-656.

9. **And of a transient date**, and quickly passed away and perished.

11. **breath**, the vital principle; the Latin *anima* or *spiritus*, the breath of life.

12. **the wiry grate**, the bars of his cage.

13. **gentle** is, of course, ironical. For *swain*, cf. note, p. 97, l. 30.

16. **express**, show, inflict.

18. **Had been**, *i.e.* should have been.

THE PINEAPPLE AND THE BEE.

INTRODUCTION.

This poem was first published in *Poems*, 1782. In a letter enclosing it to Hill, October 2, 1779, Cowper writes: "The newspaper informs me of the arrival of the Jamaica fleet. I hope it imports some pineapple plants for me. I have a good frame and a good bed prepared to receive them. I send you annexed a fable, in which the pineapple makes a figure, and shall be glad if you like the taste of it. Two pair of soles, with shrimps, which arrived last night, demand my acknowledgments. You have heard that when Arion performed upon the harp, the fish followed him. I really have no design to fiddle you out of more fish, but if you should esteem my verses worthy of such a price, though I shall never be so renowned as he was, I shall think myself equally indebted to the muse that helps me." The poet took to rearing pineapples in 1778, when "Mr. Wright's gardener presented him with six fruiting pines, which he put into a bark bed" (*To Unwin*, December 3). Cowper wrote another poem, with a somewhat different moral, under the heading *The Bee and the Pineapple*, which he apparently threw aside and intended for destruction. It was first printed in *The Universal Review* for June, 1890, in an article entitled "Unpublished MSS. of the Poet Cowper." For its interest in connexion with the present poem I quote it in full.

> "A bee allured by the perfume
> Of a rich pineapple in bloom,
> Found it within a frame enclosed,
> And licked the glass that interposed.
> Blossoms of apricot and peach,
> The flowers that blowed within his reach,
> Were arrant drugs compared with that
> He strove so vainly to get at.
> No rose could yield so rare a treat,
> Nor jessamine were half so sweet.
> The gardener saw this much-ado
> (The gardener was the master too),
> And thus he said : ' Poor restless bee !
> I learn philosophy from thee.
> I learn how just it is and wise
> To use what providence supplies,
> To leave fine titles, Lordships, Graces,
> Rich pensions, dignities, and places—
> Those gifts of a superior kind—
> To those for whom they were designed.

> I learn that comfort dwells alone
> In that which Heaven has made our own,
> That fools incur no greater pain
> Than pleasure coveted in vain.'"

NOTES.

2. **in blow**, in blowing, in bloom. Cf. "in wear" in *Report of an Adjudged Case*, 11.

8. **trunk**, proboscis.

12. **trimmed**, directed.

13. **Methinks**. *Thinks* in *methinks* ('it seems to me') means 'seems' (O.E. *thincan*, to appear), and is a different verb from 'I think' (O.E. *thencan*, to think).

17. **the spring of**, the origin of, the incentive to.

19. **Cynthio**. The name is used to represent any man of fashion. Cf. the use of "Hodge" for a rustic in *A Fable*, 24.

ogles, glances at sideways, casts sheep's eyes upon.

20. **The nymph**. See note, p. 96, l. 1.

glasses, the window-glasses in either door of the chariot.

24. **showglass**, the glazed case in which jewellery is exposed for sale.

fraught, 'laden,' is a shortened form of *fraughted* from a verb 'to fraught,' another form of 'to freight,' with past part. *freighted*.

36. **Can gather**, etc. The good and wise are not tempted by fine and showy things; they can derive satisfaction and enjoyment from the humblest objects.

THE JACKDAW.

INTRODUCTION.

This translation from Bourne was first published along with *The Glow-worm*, *The Cricket*, and *The Parrot*, in *Poems*, 1782. Vincent Bourne was assistant-master at Westminster School in Cowper's time, and published one or two volumes of Latin poems, twenty-seven of which the poet translated into English verse. Bourne died in 1747. In a letter to Unwin, May 23, 1781, Cowper writes: "I love the memory of Vinny Bourne... His humour is entirely original; he can speak of a magpie or a cat in terms so exquisitely appropriated to the character he draws, that one would suppose him animated by the spirit of the creature he describes. And with all this drollery there is a mixture of rational, and even religious reflection at times : and always an air of pleasantry, good-nature, and humanity, that makes him, in my mind, one of the most amiable writers in the world."

NOTES.

4. **the church.** "Church," in reference to the jackdaw, is the building, on the steeple of which he perches ; in reference to the bishop, it means the ecclesiastical establishment, in which he has a snug and lucrative post. Cowper, both in his poetry and his letters, is frequent in his attacks upon the clergy of his day. "Certainly," writes Canon Benham, "no man ever disliked bishops more cordially ; and as one looks over the list of that period, there seems little reason why he should have held them in veneration." The "bishop" does not figure in the original.

6. **dormitory,** *i.e.* he sometimes goes to sleep on his perch.

7. **a plate,** the vane or weather-cock.

9. **the weather,** the wind.

10. **Look up,** if you look up; see note, p. 104, l. 133.

12. **the rather,** so much more. This *the* is the old instrumental case of *the* used as a demonstrative, as in "*The* more *the* better."

13. **speculative height,** height from which he can view and contemplate everything. The phrase is a reminiscence of Milton's "specular mount" (*Par. Regained,* iv. 236).

14. **wings his ... flight.** *Flight* is to be parsed as a partially cognate object of the verb 'wings'; *i.e.* it is cognate in meaning but not in form. Compare 'to sleep a sleep' with 'to sleep a wink' (*The Retired Cat,* 75), and see note, p. 110, l. 31.

15. **securely,** unconcernedly. This meaning seems best to agree with the original. The "secure" of l. 18 may then be taken in the sense of 'safe.' Cf. note, p. 141, l. 14.

16. **raree-show,** a contraction of 'rarity-show,' a show of things rare or wonderful carried about in a box by a showman. Among the contents of a raree-show of the sixteenth century, Caulfield enumerates fighting fleas, a snake, and a tame hedgehog. The toys or vanities that occupy the attention of mankind are alluded to. Cf. *The Valediction,* 34.

20. **future,** possible, contingent.

23. **philosophic,** calmly contemplative.

25. **roundabout,** a horizontal revolving frame fitted with small wooden horses on which children ride at fairs, etc. The world is represented as full of change and revolution, like a merry-go-round at a fair, carrying with it the heterogeneous multitude of its inhabitants—clergy, soldiers, doctors, lawyers.

26. motley here may have the double sense of 'varied, hetero-geneous' and 'fantastic, buffoon-like,' motley or parti-coloured dress being the garb of court fools or jesters.

rout, crowd; cf. note to p. 101, l. 33.

33. 'em is not a contraction of *them*, but is equivalent to *hem*, the old dative and accusative plural of *he*.

36. such a head, a sensible, "philosophic pate," like yours. In *To Unwin*, May 23, 1781, Cowper writes: "That is epigram-matic and witty in Latin, which would be perfectly insipid in English; and a translator of Bourne would frequently find him-self obliged to supply what is called the turn ... To quote myself, you will find, in comparing the Jackdaw with the original, that I was obliged to sharpen a point which, though smart enough in the Latin, would, in English, have appeared as plain and as blunt as the tag of a lace." The "point" he "sharpened" seems to refer to this last line, which is an addition to the original.

THE CRICKET.

INTRODUCTION.

See Introduction to the previous poem. There is a well-known sonnet on the Cricket by Leigh Hunt. Cowper's lines have all the delicate grace of Anacreontic verse, in imitation of which the original is written.

NOTES.

1. **inmate,** dweller in my house.

2. **hearth.** Cf. Milton, *Il Penseroso*, 81, 82:

> "Far from all resort of mirth,
> Save the cricket on the *hearth*."

4. **harbinger of good.** In folklore, the cricket was supposed to bring good luck to a house, and to kill it was a deed of ill omen. *Harbinger* is M.E. *herbergeour*, one who goes before to provide lodgings for a host or army (from *har-bour*, lit. 'host-shelter'), and so 'forerunner' or 'prognosticator.'

6. **more soft,** *i.e.* softer and sweeter than before.

8. **a strain,** viz., this poem in your praise.

9. **Thus thy praise,** etc., *i.e.* you shall be praised as being an inoffensive welcome guest.

11. **on the scout.** See note, p. 97, l. 34.

12. **curious**, prying, inquisitive; the Latin original has *mures curiosi*, 'inquisitive mice.'

17. **they**, *i.e.* the grasshoppers.

22. **the winter long**, for the whole length of the winter; cf. 'All day long' (p. 70, l. 1). *Long* is an adverb, and *winter* is an adverbial objective modifying it.

27. **extend thy span**, etc. The meaning is that, since the cheerful life is the only true life, the cricket's songful existence is really longer than that of man, spent in "repining discontent." Cf. *To Rose*, June 23, 1788 : "We can only bo said truly to have lived, while we have been profitably employed. Alas, then ! making the necessary deductions, how short is life."

32. **Half a span**, a very short space of time. "Thy span" in l. 27 means "thy brief life."

BOADICEA.

INTRODUCTION.

This ode was first published in *Poems*, 1782, and is stated to have been written two years earlier, just after the poet had read the account given of Boadicea in Hume's *History of England*. The Queen, after her scourging by the Romans, is represented as consulting the Druids—who, however, had recently been exterminated by the Romans. The aged priest foretells the downfall of Rome and the future empire of her posterity. Cowper uses a poet's license in dealing with the historical facts, for the present inhabitants of Britain are mainly of Anglo-Saxon race, and can hardly be called the posterity of the ancient Britons. Tennyson's poem *Boädicea*, among his "Experiments," forms a good illustration of Cowper's verses.

In A.D. 47, the Iceni (Norfolk), under their king Prasutagus, made submission to the Romans, and he, upon his death, bequeathed his dominions to the Republic, in the hope of thus securing consideration for his family. But his widowed queen Boadicea, suspected perhaps of concealing his treasure, was scourged with rods by the Roman authorities, and his daughters were treated with contumely. Maddened by her wrongs in A.D. 61, she raised the standard of revolt, and many of the other tribes joining the Iceni, they surprised and captured the Roman colonies of Camulodunum (Colchester), Verulamium (St. Albans), and Londinium, and slaughtered many thousands of the Roman inhabitants. But the Roman general, Suetonius, advanced to the neighbourhood of Camulodunum, and there, in spite of the efforts of Boadicea, who drove her car from rank to rank of her countrymen, with her daughters beside her, declaring the outrage

H

she had endured and calling for vengeance, the Iceni were defeated in a great battle, and 80,000 of them slain. Boadicea herself, rather than fall into the hands of the enraged conqueror, put an end to her life by poison.

NOTES.

2. rods. The Romans used rods for scourging, a favourite mode of punishment with them. The Roman provincial governor had his attendant lictors, who carried a bundle of rods with an axe in the middle, indicating that he had the power of scourging and of inflicting capital punishment.

4. her country's gods. In the Druidical system, the objects of nature were identified with the memory of deceased heroes, and the sun and stars, the thunder and the whirlwind, were worshipped as the visible representatives of superior beings. Thus the sun-god was Belenus; Taranis was the wielder of the thunderbolt; Hesus was their god of battles; while Teutates, venerated as the patron of all their civilization, seems to have held the highest place amongst them (Merivale, *History of the Romans*, Ch. v.).

5. Sage, wise; here an adjective.

oak. The Druidical rites were performed in sacred groves of oak. Cf. Lucan's apostrophe to the Druids (*Phars.* i. 445-457): *Nemora alta remotis Incolitis lucis,* 'Ye abide in the silvan recesses of sequestered groves.' The attempt to connect *Druid* with Gael. *darach*, Welsh *derw*, an oak, is, says Skeat, by no means convincing.

6. the Druid. The Druids were very powerful in Britain. They were not only priests, but also judges, bards, and teachers of the youth of the country.

7. burning word, passionate word. So Gray (*Progress of Poesy,* 110) represents Fancy as scattering

"Thoughts that breathe and words that *burn.*"

Lines 7 and 8 form an absolute clause.

9. if = 'although' here.

11, 12. ties ... tongues, prevents us from uttering the curses that we could otherwise speak. At the attack made upon Anglesey by the Romans, "the Druids were seen raising their hands to heaven, invoking curses on the daring invaders," which so dismayed the Romans that they at first stood motionless (Merivale, Ch. LI.).

13. that word, that statement, that prophecy.

13, 14. write ... In the blood. For the figure, cf. *Heroism,* 42.

16. **Deep ... guilt.** Her destruction shall be as complete as her wickedness has been great.

19. **kiss the ground,** be humbled, brought low. Cf. Bible, *Psalms*, lxxii. 9 : "His (Solomon's) enemies shall *lick the dust.*"

20. **the Gaul ... gates.** The Gauls, under Brennus, attacked and burnt Rome, B.C. 390 ; but that, of course, was long before this time. In A.D. 410, the Goths, under Alaric, invaded Italy and sacked Rome, and it would almost seem that Cowper confused these two events, unless he employs *Gaul* as a general name for the northern barbarians.

21. **Other Romans,** etc. Conquest and dominion were regarded by the Romans of the Republic and the Empire as their special *rôle—"Hae tibi erunt artes"*; see the whole passage, Vergil, *Aeneid,* vi. 847-853. But the modern Italians are pre-eminent in the arts of music and singing, and for the last two centuries Italy has produced the finest singers in the world. In Cowper's day, Italy was a feeble aggregation of small states ; but, since then, united under one rule, she has become one of the great powers, and Garibaldi, an Italian, is one of the most famous of modern soldiers.

25. **the progeny that springs,** etc. Rather an awkward expression for ships built of oaks grown in British forests. The allusion is to the future naval supremacy of Great Britain. The "thunder" is the cannon (cf. note, p. 117, l. 31), and the "wings" the sails of our men-of-war. Cf. Tennyson, *Boädicea,* 38-44 :

"' Fear not, isle of blowing woodland, isle of silvery parapets !
  Tho' the Roman eagle shadow thee, tho' the gathering enemy
    narrow thee,
  Thou shalt wax and he shall dwindle, thou shalt be the
    mighty one yet !
  Thine the liberty, thine the glory, thine the deeds to be
    celebrated,
  Thine the myriad-rolling ocean, light and shadow illimitable,
  Thine the lands of lasting summer, many-blossoming Para-
    dises,
  Thine the north and thine the south, and thine the *battle-
    thunder* of God.'"

29. **Regions Caesar never knew,** etc. The Romans knew nothing of America, Australia, and New Zealand ; and their eagles never flew over (*i.e.* they never invaded) India, Burmah, or South Africa besides : all of which are under the dominion of the English race ("thy posterity"). The Roman standard consisted of a pole surmounted by the silver or bronze image of an eagle with expanded wings. This bird was the recognised Roman ensign, and one of these standards was carried by every

legion. The construction of this stanza is: "Thy posterity shall sway regions (which) Caesar never knew, (regions) where his eagles never flew, none (being) as invincible as they (*i.e.* thy posterity)."

34. **Pregnant ... fire**, full of divine inspiration. The line is taken from Gray's *Elegy* (1742-1750), 46:

> "Perhaps in this neglected spot is laid
> Some heart once *pregnant with celestial fire.*"

Gray (*The Bard*, 21) has a "prophet's fire," and Shakspere (*Henry V.* I. i. 1) has "a Muse of fire."

39. **Rushed to battle**, etc. See Introduction, where it will be seen that Boadicea was not killed in the battle but poisoned herself.

40. **hurled them**, uttered them defiantly. She repeats in her own words the prophecy of the Druid.

HEROISM.

INTRODUCTION.

This poem was first published in *Poems*, 1782. It would appear from letters to Newton that *The Burning Mountain* and *Ætna* were its original titles. Writing to Newton, December 17, 1781, Cowper says: "Modern naturalists, I think, tell us that the volcano forms the mountain. I shall be charged therefore, perhaps, with an unphilosophical (*i.e.* unscientific) error in supposing that Ætna was once unconscious of intestine fires, and as lofty as at present before the commencement of the eruptions." And he proceeds to ask his correspondent "whether you think an apologetical note may be necessary; for I would not appear a dunce in matters that every review reader must needs be apprized of." Cowper, born in 1731, was twenty-five years old at the commencement of the Seven Years' War (1756-1763), which was caused by the greed of France and Austria, who leagued themselves for the partition of Prussia by a secret treaty, to which Russia, Saxony, and Sweden afterwards acceded. These too were the days of the first partition of Poland between Austria, Russia, and Prussia, which happened in 1772. An insolent self-seeking, an eagerness for territorial aggrandisement, the oppression of the weak by the strong, were the distinguishing characteristics of continental politics in the poet's time, which saw the fairest regions of Europe devastated before the march of destroying armies, the "heroism" of whose achievements Cowper knew how to estimate at its true value.

The title of this poem is, of course, bitterly ironical; cf. *Task*, v. 279-282:

"Kings
Were burnished into *heroes*, and became
The arbiters of this terraqueous swamp,
Storks among frogs, that have but croaked and died."

NOTES.

1. **Ætna's silent fire**, Mount Ætna or Etna, a volcano in Sicily. Eruptions are mentioned by Diodorus Siculus as happening as early as B.C. 1693. These eruptions recurred at intervals, and in 1669 tens of thousands of persons perished in the streams of lava which rolled over the whole country for forty days and destroyed numerous villages. In 1766 a serious eruption had occurred.

2. **the mountain yet entire**, the mountain being as yet entire—an absolute clause, like ll. 8, 12, 21, 44.

7. **unctuous**, oily, oil-producing. The word is now generally used in the metaphorical sense of ' plausible, sanctimonious.'

9. The construction is : " Her unctuous olives and her purple vines assured (*i.e.* gave confidence to) the peasant's hopes, and not in vain, (being) matured (*i.e.* ripened) in peace upon her sloping sides."

11. **on a day**, one day. *A* (= *an* = *one*) retains its full original meaning here, as in ' two of *a* trade,' ' birds of *a* feather,' ' one at *a* time,' etc. Cf. note, p. 91, l. 124.

that of the last doom, the Judgment-Day,

"When, shrivelling like a parchèd scroll,
The flaming heavens together roll ;
When louder yet, and yet more dread
Swells the high trump that wakes the dead !" (Scott.)

12. **womb.** Cf. *The Needless Alarm*, 86, and *Task*, ii. 88-90 :
" Her hollow *womb*,
Conceiving thunders, through a thousand deeps
And fiery caverns, roars beneath his foot."
Also notes to ll. 13, 17 below.

13. **teemed**, brought forth, was fruitful. The verb *teem* is formed from the noun *team*, 'progeny, a set, a row,' as in 'a *team* of horses. Cf. Shaks. *1 Henry IV*. III. i. 27-33 :
" Diseased nature oftentimes breaks forth
In strange eruptions ; oft the *teeming* earth
Is with a kind of colic pinch'd and vex'd
By the imprisoning of unruly wind

> Within her womb ; which, for enlargement striving,
> Shakes the old beldam earth and topples down
> Steeples and moss-grown towers."

15. **the vapours**, the clouds of smoke from the volcano.

16. **hang their horrors.** Cf. Milton, *Par. Lost*, ii. 174-178 :

> " What if all
> Her stores were open'd, and this firmament
> Of Hell should spout her cataracts of fire,
> *Impendent horrors*, threatening hideous fall
> One day upon our heads."

17. **Stygian**, black, gloomy, like the night of the infernal regions. The *Styx* was one of the rivers of the Greek Hades, so that *Stygian* means 'hellish.' Cf. Milton, *Comus*, 131-133 :

> " When the dragon womb
> Of *Stygian* darkness spets her thickest gloom,
> And makes one *blot* of all the air."

And *Task*, iii. 738 (of London chimneys) :

> "Whose *Stygian* throats breathe darkness all day long."

19. **powers of song**, heights of poetic description.

20. **trace the torrent**, give an account of the course of the torrent of lava.

21. **in the van**, in front of it. *Van* is short for *vanguard*, and is the French *avant*, Lat. *ab ante*, from in front.

24. **year**, climate.

26. **uninformed**, unmoulded by internal forces, uninspired with life, chaotic. Cf. Milton, *Par. Lost*, iii. 593, 594 (of the sun) :

> "Not all parts like, but all alike *inform'd*
> With radiant light, as glowing iron with fire."

And Dryden, *Absalom and Achitophel*, Part i., 156-158 :

> " A fiery soul, which working out its way,
> Fretted the pigmy body to decay,
> And o'er-*informed* the tenement of clay."

31. **spiry myrtle.** Cowper employs the same epithet in *Tas* III. 570 :

> " The *spiry* myrtle with unwithering leaf
> Shines there, and flourishes."

Wordsworth applies the epithet to the trees in *Laodamia*, last stanza : " A knot of *spiry* trees."

32. **ruminating flocks.** So Milton (*Comus*, 540) has "the chewing flocks," and in *Anti-Thelypthora*, 78, we find "the ruminating sheep."

33. **precarious**, lit. ' obtained by prayer, obtained as a favour,' hence ' uncertain ' ; Lat. *precari*, to pray.

35. **self-same.** See note, p. 71, l. 19.

39. **swains,** 'poetical' for *peasants*; cf. *Mrs. Throckmorton's Bullfinch*, 30.

scene, prospect, landscape.

41. **the lure of honour,** the attraction of winning honour.

42. **Who write ... cause,** who cause bloodshed in the defence of your cause. The same metaphor occurs in *Boadicea*, 13, 14.

43. **Who strike ... defence,** who are the first to attack, and then say that they fought only in self-defence.

44. **Glory ... pretence.** The poet in *Table Talk*, 9-38, distinguishes between the leader who, fighting for Justice,

> "In Honour's field advancing the firm foot,
> Plants it upon the line that Justice draws,
> And will prevail or perish in her cause,"

and the leader who fights for Glory—

> "The wretch, to naught but his ambition true,
> Who for the sake of filling with one blast
> The posthorns of all Europe, lays her waste."

47. **Fast,** 'close'; an adverb. Cf. note, p. 117, l. 4. With this passage cf. *Task*, i. 609, 610:

> "War followed for revenge, or to supplant
> The envied tenants of some happier spot";

and *Ib.*, v. 225-228:

> "Industry in some
> To improve and cultivate their just demesne,
> Made others covet what they saw so fair.
> Thus war began on earth."

50. **Studious of peace,** desirous of peace, making peace their aim. Cf. Milton, *Par. Lost*, 107: "The *study* of revenge."

53. **legions,** 'troops.' The Roman 'legion' was about the equivalent of our 'battalion.'

58. **behind a wilderness.** See Introduction.

59. **her first-born son,** *i.e.* the earliest result of famine is pestilence. A similar metaphor is seen in 'Necessity is the mother of Invention,' and in Tennyson's

> "Raw Haste, half-sister to Delay."

Cf. also note, p. 110, l. 38.

60. **begun.** "Past Indicative tenses in *u* were common in the seventeenth century" (Abbott, *Shaks. Gr.*), and they survived into the eighteenth. *Sang* does not occur in Shakspere, while *sung* is common, and *sprang* is less common than *sprung*. Milton too writes *sprung* as a past tense (*Par. Lost*, i. 331). We find *begun* for *began* in *Hamlet*, III. ii. 220. Cowper has the preterite

begun only here, but he has *sung* three times (cf. note, p. 128, l. 23), and *sprung* once (cf. note, p. 96, l. 8).

63. **train**, 'retinue, accompaniment,' from Fr. *train*, contracted from *tragimen*, derived from *tragere* = Lat. *trahere*, to draw.

66. **What scourges are the gods.** Alaric (see note, p. 79, l. 20), called himself 'The Scourge of God'; and cf. *Task*, v. 190-192:

> "Heroes, whose infirm and baby minds
> Are gratified with mischief, and who spoil,
> Because men suffer it, their toy the world.".

Also Milton, *Par. Lost*, xi. 689-697:

> "For in those days might only shall be admired,
> And valour and heroic virtue called;
> To overcome in battle, and subdue
> Nations, and bring home spoils with infinite
> Man-slaughter, shall be held the highest pitch
> Of human glory, and for glory done
> Of triumph, to be styl'd great conquerors,
> Patrons of mankind, *gods*, and *sons of gods*;
> Destroyers rightlier call'd, and plagues of men."

And *Task*, v. 266 (of the 'hero'):

> "They *demi-deify* and fume him so."

69. **Plies ... toil**, exerts all his powers of industrious work.

70. **Gleans ... spoil**, gathers together what little is left undestroyed in the widespread devastation.

74. **Renew ... part**, cause them to be again attacked by their former conqueror.

76. **at the door**, close at hand, imminent. Cf. Milton, *Lycidas*, 130: "That two-handed engine *at the door*."

77. **laurelled heroes.** Among the Romans victorious generals, in triumphal processions, wore laurel crowns on their head, and carried laurel branches in their hands, while their lictors' fasces (bundles of rods) were bound with laurel. Hence, in modern times, the laurel is regarded as the symbol of victory. Cf. *Task*, vi. 939: "The *laurels* that a Caesar reaps."

79. **stripped of her embroidered robe.** Cf. ll. 57, 58 above. And *Task*, v. 107: "The *embroidered* banks," and Milton, *Lycidas*, 148: "Every flower that sad *embroidery* wears." *Broider* (without the prefix) is from Fr. *broder, border*, from *bord*, edge, and meant originally 'to work on the edge,' hence, 'to ornament with needlework.'

81. **bar**, a rail; hence, a railed enclosure; and so such an enclosure in a court of law, where prisoners were placed to have judgment passed upon them. Cf. *Progress of Error*, 28:

> "Say to what *bar* amenable were man?"

82. **destroyers.** See note to l. 66 above—"Destroyers rightlier called."

you ... ye. The old distinction between *ye* and *you—ye* being exclusively nominative, and *you* dative and accusative—happens to be preserved here. It is observed in the Bible, but not by Elizabethan or later authors.

86. **No created ... blood.** Tennyson (*Lancelot and Elaine*, 306, 307) represents King Arthur at the battle of Badon Hill as standing
"High on a heap of slain, from spur to *plume*
Red as the rising sun with heathen blood."

88. With this line compare l. 76.

89. **tyrants hate in vain.** For the unsuccessful attempt of the continental powers to crush Great Britain, cf. General Introduction, pp. xii., xiii.

90. **a George's,** *i.e.* George III., who reigned from 1760 to 1820.

EPISTLE TO JOSEPH HILL.

INTRODUCTION.

This poem was appended, along with *Tirocinium* and *John Gilpin*, to the *Task* on its first publication in 1785. In a postscript to a letter to Unwin, November 20, 1784, Cowper says: "You will find also an Epistle to Joseph Hill, Esq., which I wrote on Wednesday last ; a tribute so due that I must have disgraced myself had I not paid it. He ever serves me in all that he can, though he has not seen me, these twenty years."

Joseph Hill, the "Josephus" or "'Sephus" of the Letters, was Cowper's schoolfellow at Westminster, and one of the seven members of the Nonsense Club, and a man of some humour. "I often think," writes the poet to him (June 9, 1786), "of your most heroic line, written at one of our meetings, and especially think of it when I am translating Homer :

' To whom replied the Devil yard-long-tailed.'

There was never anything more truly Grecian than that triple epithet ; and were it possible to introduce it into either *Iliad* or *Odyssey* I should certainly steal it." Hill was a lawyer and a man of good business habits, and, greatly to the benefit of the poet, took charge of his finances. He survived him, and died at an advanced age.

NOTES.

1. **Five and twenty years ago.** In 1752 Cowper became a law-student in chambers in the Middle Temple, and was called to the

bar in 1754. In 1759 he removed to the Inner Temple. It was during this Temple period that the "frequent intercourse" with Hill occurred, though later on Hill seems to have paid him a visit at Huntingdon. A letter to Hill, December 7, 1782, pleasantly recalls an incident of this intercourse, and then Cowper remarks: "This is the nineteenth winter since I saw you in this situation." This personal intimacy ended with the poet's removal to St. Albans in 1763.

4, 5. to cheat A tedious hour, to make it pass quickly and pleasantly. Cf. *Task*, iii. 362, "Happy to *deceive* the time, Not waste it"; and *Ib*. iv. 164, "The poet's or historian's page etc. *Beguile* the night"; and the Latin *fallere noctem*, 'to deceive the night.'

8. Good lack, a variant of alack (= ah! lack!), "good" being used as in 'Good Heavens!' *Lack* is probably M.E. *lak*, loss, failure. Cf. *John Gilpin*, 61.

14. wane, decline. *Want* comes from the same root.

18. stood the touch, been tested and found genuine. The "touch-stone," or Lydian stone, a kind of basalt, was so called because gold was touched with it, and its purity estimated according to the mark left by the metal. Cf. Shaks. *Richard III.* IV. ii. 8, 9:

> "O Buckingham, now do I play the *touch*,
>   To try if thou be current gold indeed."

And *1 Henry IV.* IV. iv. 8-10:

> "A day
> Wherein the fortune of ten thousand men
> Must bide the *touch*."

And Montrose, *My Dear and Only Love*:

> "He either fears his fate too much,
>   Or his deserts are small,
> That dares not put it to the *touch*,
>   To gain or lose it all.'

19. gold they seemed. Cowper had probably Thurlow and Colman in his mind; see Introduction to *The Valediction*, p. 119.

24. turning short about, turning round abruptly.

27. An please you, if it please you. *And* was formerly used in the sense of *if*, *i.e.* it added something conditionally, so that 'I will not go out *and* it rains'= I will not go out *if* it rains. Then, in order to mark off this use of *and* from the ordinary use, the final *d* was dropt and *and* became an. Subsequently, when this old force of *an* began to be forgotten, *if* was appended to explain it, and we get *an if*.

29. marry, a corruption of "By (the Virgin) Mary." Cf. *zounds* (= God's wounds).

32. I knew the man. It is doubtful for whom "Horatio" was meant. Perhaps for the Rev. Roger Donne, his uncle at Catfield, in Norfolk, whose children were his playmates as a boy, and with whom he spent his holidays.

34. somewhat...close, something strongly irritated him; stung him to the quick. *Somewhat* is not now used as a pronoun, only as an adverb. Cf. Cowper's *Letters, To Hurdis*, February 23, 1793: "Mrs. Unwin and I, crossing a brook, saw *somewhat* at the bottom of the water which had the appearance of a flower"; and Bible, *Revelation*, ii. 4: "I have *somewhat* against thee, because thou hast left thy first love."

36. his confidence...betrayed, an absolute clause, with *being* understood.

40. in my mind, in my opinion.

55. hard...measure, severe penalty, harsh reckoning. The phrase is Scriptural; cf. Bible, *Matthew*, vii. 2: "With what measure ye mete, it shall be measured to you again."

57. our triple state, our government by King, Lords, and Commons, known as the three estates of the realm.

58. Some few, etc. See note to l. 19 above.

JOHN GILPIN.

INTRODUCTION.

One evening in October, 1782, Lady Austen endeavoured to enliven Cowper's low spirits by recounting the story of John Gilpin, "which," she said, "had been told her in her childhood." During the night peals of laughter were heard issuing from his bedroom, and by morning he had turned the tale into a rough outline of this ballad. After being polished and improved, it was sent to Unwin, who declared that it made him "laugh tears," and who soon after (November 4) received the poet's permission to print it, only without the author's name; and it accordingly appeared in the *Public Advertiser* of November 14, 1782. Writing to Unwin on November 18 of the same year, Cowper says: "I little thought when I was writing the history of John Gilpin that he would appear in print. I intended to laugh, and to make two or three others laugh, of whom you were one. But now all the world laughs, at least if they have the same relish for a tale ridiculous in itself, and quaintly told, as we have." In a letter to Unwin, May 8, 1784, we find *John Gilpin* spoken of as having been "hacknied in every magazine, in every newspaper, and in every street"; and in a subsequent letter (October 20, 1784) to the same correspondent, with reference to the proposal of appending the ballad to his second volume,

Cowper writes: "He (John Gilpin) has made a good deal of noise in the world, and perhaps it may not be amiss to show, that though I write generally with a serious intention, I know how to be occasionally merry." In 1785 the ballad, in its newspaper form, came under the notice of Richard Sharp— "Conversation Sharp," as he was called—who showed it to John Henderson, the actor, and suggested that he should include it in the public readings he was then giving at Freemason's Hall. Overflowing audiences, Mrs. Siddons among them, greeted its delivery with laughter and applause, and the ballad became town talk. "Gilpin," says Southey, "passing at full stretch by the Bell at Edmonton, was to be seen in all print shops. One printseller sold six thousand. What had succeeded so well in London was repeated with equal success on provincial stages, and the ballad became in the highest degree popular before the author's name was known." It was doubtless owing to this popularity that it was finally decided to include *John Gilpin* in the *Task* volume, published in 1785.

The "famous horseman" has been variously identified with a Mr. John Beyer, a linendraper living in Cheapside, who died in 1791 at the age of 98; and with a certain John Gilpin, apprenticed to a linendraper in Fleet Street, who lived in a house in Cheapside, and died in 1750, leaving two daughters, who, with a son who died previously, would make up the "children three" of the ballad.

Cowper tells us (*To Unwin*, May 8, 1784) that he was recommended by a lady to write a sequel to *John Gilpin*, but "had more prudence than to take her counsel.' A short paper entitled "Mrs. Gilpin riding to Edmonton,' headed by a rude woodcut of a woman in a poke-bonnet sitting on a stile, appears in Hone's *Table Book* (1827-28) Vol. II., in which three stanzas of a supposed episode or sequel to *John Gilpin* are fathered upon Cowper; for the evidence is complete that the piece is a *feu d'esprit* by Charles Lamb, who was living at Enfield, near Edmonton, at the time, and who was buried in Edmonton Churchyard.

It is not improbable that Cowper had his own horsemanship in mind when he wrote *John Gilpin*, for he writes to Unwin (May, 1781) that he is sure that Nature "did not design me for a horseman"; and remarks: "I should comfort myself with the thought that I had not a beast under me whose walk would seem tedious, whose trot would jumble me (cf. l. 84), and whose gallop might throw me into a ditch."

NOTES.

3. train-band. The train-bands were a militia enrolled for the protection of the city of London. They consisted of twelve regiments of infantry and two regiments of cavalry, and their drilling-place was Mile-End. They were ridiculed by the Cavaliers at the outbreak of the Civil War of 1642, as being composed of apprentices, artizans, and shopkeepers, but they did good service in the early battles of the war. They were, in consequence, disbanded by Charles II., but were afterwards reorganised, and continued for many years. *Trainband* is short for "trained band," like *driftwood* for "drifted wood," *lock-jaw* for "locked-jaw," etc. Green (*Hist. of the Eng. People*, pp. 546, 548), has both "Trained Bands" and "trainbands."

eke, 'also,' from the verb *eke*, to augment, cognate with Lat. *augere.* Cf. 'to eke out a living,' *i.e.* to supply one's daily needs. See l. 92 below.

5. her dear, her dear one, her husband. Cf. *The Lily and the Rose*, 26, "The fairest British *fair*," and note.

10. repair. See note, p. 68, l. 52. Here we have the *pair* of "repair" rhyming with *pair* (line 12). Milton once and Spenser occasionally make a word rhyme with itself, when used in differing senses. Cf. Milton, *Sonnets*, iv. 5, 8: "Ruth" (the name) and "ruth" compassion); Spenser, *Faerie Queene*, I. i. 39. 4, 7: "steepe" (abrupt) and "steepe" (soak).

11. the Bell at Edmonton. The Bell inn at Edmonton, a village in Middlesex, near Enfield, about sixty-five miles north of London.

12. All is an adverb here (as in l. 39 below), and means 'altogether, just.' It is often so used in ballad poetry ; cf. Coleridge, *Ancient Mariner*, Part II., st. 7: "*All* in a hot and copper sky."

16. we, playfully for 'us,' to rhyme with "three." Similarly Cowper's rhyming letter to Newton (July 12, 1781) ends "himself and he has visited *we* "

19. dear. See note to l. 5 above.

23. the calender. The more correct form would be *calendrer, i.e. calenderer,* one whose trade it is to smooth and trim woollen cloth by the use of a *calender,* a machine consisting of two rollers or cylinders in near contact with each other, between which the cloth was passed and so subjected to powerful pressure. *Calender* is a doublet of *cylinder,* from a Greek word, κυλίνδειν, meaning 'to roll.'

26. for that, because that, since. The expression is common in Elizabethan English.

36. she was proud. Cf. the disappointed "pride" of Mesdames Raddle and Cluppins, whose cabriolet "was stayed three doors off" Mrs. Bardell's dwelling—"Here was a mean and low way of arriving at a friend's house!" (Dickens, *Pickwick Papers*, Chap. xlvi.)

39. all agog, very eager. *A-gog* = 'in eagerness'; cf. Beaumont and Fletcher, *Wit without Money*, iii. 1 : "You have put me in such a *gog* of going, I would not stay for all the world."

40. through thick and thin, *i.e.* anywhere whatever ; through all obstacles. In "Old English Legends" of 1360, occurs "Fiends will not cease *for thin ne thick*" (*i.e.* for any cause). The phrase also occurs in Chaucer, *Cant. Tales*, ii. 121. In "thick and thin" there is an ellipse of the noun (things, places) as in Wordsworth's "Through *rough* and *smooth* she trips along" (*Lucy Gray*). Cf. Milton, *Par. Lost*, ii. 948, where Satan "pursues his way"—

"O'er bog or steep, through *strait, rough, dense* or *rare*.

44. Cheapside. A street in the City of London. In old times it was a market-place, and contained a cross, pulled down by the Puritans in 1645. See Introduction.

49. saddle-tree, the wooden frame of the saddle, here equivalent to the saddle itself. *Tree* has its older meaning of 'wood' here : cf. Spenser's *treën*, 'wooden.'

58. suited to their mind, provided with wares that pleased them.

59. Betty, a short form of Eliza*beth* ; here the servant-maid's name. In older English *Bete* (our *Betty*) is used as short for *Beatrix*.

61. "Good lack." See note, p. 86, l. 8.

quoth, said. The simple form of the verb is seen in the compound 'be*queath*.'

64. exercise, drill. As a captain (l. 3) of the city militia, he wore a sword.

69. ear, handle.

74. top to toe, head to foot.

84. galled him in his seat, made him feel sore by jolting him against the saddle. Cf. Introduction, *ad fin.*

85. "Fair and softly." Addressed to his horse to induce him to go at a gentler pace. The phrase first occurs in Tyndale. Shakspere uses 'soft' as an interjection, in the sense of 'hush' or 'stay ; cf. *Romeo and Juliet*, II. ii. 2 : "But, *soft*! what light through yonder window breaks?"

John he cried. In ballad style for 'John cried.' For this reduplication of the subject, cf. Shakspere, *1 Henry IV.* III. ii. 60 : "The skipping *king he* ambled up and down."

89. needs, of need, of necessity—an adverb which is an old genitive case ; cf. *always, sometimes, unawares.*

97. neck or nought, in reckless fashion ; not caring whether he risked his neck or risked nothing ; cf. l. 40 and note. The humour of the passage consists in the fact that Gilpin's reckless daring was involuntary.

100. **running such a rig**, playing such a prank. *Rig* is connected with *wriggle*.

108. **said or** (rather) **sung**, told, or, to speak more exactly, told in verse.

115. **"He carries weight."** In horse-racing, superior horses are handicapped by being made to carry additional weight. John Gilpin's "race" here would be looked upon as a "time race," since he was riding alone, and not with others, as in l. 244 below.

116. **a thousand pound.** Note the omission of the sign of the plural; similarly we say 'two *dozen*,' 'four *pair*.' Keble (*Christian Year*) has "Saints, parted by a thousand *year*."

119. **in a trice**, quickly, suddenly. *Trice* is the Span. *tris*, the noise made by the breaking of glass; so that 'in a trice' = the vulgar 'in a crack.' Cf. L 223 below.

turnpike-men. Called the 'toll-men' in l. 243 below. A *turnpike* is a toll-gate, or gate set across a road to stop those liable to pay toll for the use of the road, the "turnpike-men" being those who collected the tolls, but who on this occasion threw open their gates so as not to hinder the supposed race. The name was given to the toll-gate, because it took the place of the old turnstile, which was made with four horizontal *pikes* or arms, which *turned* or revolved on the top of a post. Toll-gates were first set up in 1663, and from time to time Acts of Parliament were passed abolishing them.

122. **reeking**, steaming, perspiring.

124. **at a blow**, 'at one blow.' cf. note, p. 81, l. 11. The bottles swung round and collided behind him.

128. **As they had** etc., as though they had been basted. See note, p. 109, L 16. To *baste* is to drop fat over meat while it is being roasted.

133. **Islington.** At this time a village on the outskirts of London. The epithet "merry" is in old ballad style, as in 'merry England,' 'merry Carlisle' (Scott, *Lay of the Last Minstrel*), 'merry men' (of forest outlaws). *Gay* is similarly used in l. 136 below.

134. **gambols he did play.** See note, p. 75, l. 14.

135. **the Wash**, apparently the name given to a pool or brook that crossed the road near Edmonton.

139. **trundling**, twirling, revolving. A mop is trundled after use to make the moisture fly out of it. Cf. '*trundle*-bed,' a bed running on wheels.

142. balcony here is accented on the second syllable (*balcóny*), the common pronunciation in Cowper's day. The poet Rogers, a contemporary of Cowper, says : "*Cóntemplate* is bad enough, but *bálcony* makes me sick." Byron also writes *balcóny*. Similarly Cowper has *siníster, enérvate, promúlgate*, in which we now throw the accent a syllable further back. On the other hand, he has *phlégmatic, cónsummate*, and *splénetic*. Cf. note, p. 131, l. 27.

149. a whit, a bit, at all. *Whit* (= *wiht*) is the same word as *wight*, (1) a person, (2) a thing. Cf. *aught* (= a whit) and *naught* (= no whit).

151. For why ? is a mistaken rendering of the O. E. form *forwhy* (= because), in which *why* is the old instrumental case of *who*. Cf. l. 212 below.

152. Ware, a small town in Hertfordshire, once famous for its " Great Bed," measuring twelve feet in length and breadth.

162. trim, plight, condition.

172. guise, way, manner ; a doublet of the noun *wise*, as in 'like*wise*.'

176. upon the road. The jest consists in the double sense of the phrase, viz., (1) lying upon the road, (2) journeying hitherwards.

178. in merry pin, 'in a merry mood.' The phrase is generally attributed to the old custom, said to have been introduced by Dunstan, of having *pins* or pegs fixed at intervals inside tankards, to regulate the amount each person in the company should drink. Cf. Nash, *Pierce Penilesse* : "King Edgar, because his subjects should not offend in swilling and bibbing, as they did, caused certaine yron cups to be chayned to everie fountaine and wells-side, and at everie vintner's doore, with yron *pins* in them, to stint everie man how much he should drinke ; and he that went beyond one of those pins forfeyted a pennie for everie draught." So that he who drank more than his share might be described as "in (or on) a merry pin." But probably *pin* in this phrase is merely used for 'point' or 'position,' and so 'condition.' Thus Chaucer, *Cant. Tales*, ii. 282, has, 'Your herte hongeth on a joly *pin*"; and in the Percy Folio MS., Vol. II., p. 297, l. 34, we find :

> "But I have sett her on such a *pinn*,
> King Adler shall her never winne,"

i.e. 'I have placed her in such a position.' Cf. *Ibid., Fryar and Boye*, 484 : "Each sett *on a mery pin*."

192. case, condition.

204. sing. Playfully for 'bray.'

205. as he. See l. 128 above and note.

214. **posting**, riding swiftly. Cf. '*post*-haste.' To *post* is lit. to travel by *posts* or stages, using relays of horses.

222. **amain**, 'at full speed'; lit. 'with full power,' since *a* = 'on' or 'with,' and *main* = 'strength,' as in 'with might and *main*.'

232. **lumbering**, rumbling. *Lumber* is probably an imitative word expressive of the noise made by the motion of a heavy body, and cognate with *lump* and *clumsy*.

236. **hue and cry**, the loud outcry with which felons were pursued in old times. Cf. Scott, *Kenilworth*, xxiv.: "'Harro and help, and *hue and cry*, every true man!' said the mercer; 'I am withstood in seeking to recover mine own.'" Note that *hue* (connected with *hoot*) is used only in this phrase.

249. **Long live the king!** Similarly the last stanza of the ballad of Chevy Chase runs:

> "*God save our king* and bless this land
> With plenty, joy, and peace;
> And grant henceforth that foul debate
> 'Twixt noblemen may cease."

THE POPLAR FIELD.

INTRODUCTION.

This poem is generally supposed to have been written near the close of 1784, since, in a letter to Unwin, January 15, 1785, Cowper writes of Nichols (the editor of the *Gentleman's Magazine*), as "having at present a small piece of mine in his hands, not yet printed (it is called the Poplar Field, and I suppose you have it)." See, however, the note to l. 5 below. It was first published in that Magazine for January, 1785, and afterwards included in *Poems*, 1800. In a letter to Lady Hesketh, May 1, 1786, the poet writes: "There was, indeed, some time since, in a neighbouring parish called Lavendon, a field, one side of which formed a terrace, and the other was planted with poplars, at whose foot ran the Ouse, that I used to account a little paradise: but the poplars have been felled, and the scene has suffered so much by the loss, that though still in point of prospect beautiful, it has not charms sufficient to attract me now. A certain poet wrote a copy of verses on this melancholy occasion, which, though they have been printed, I dare say you never saw." The poplar-field, known as "Lynch Close," stood near Lavendon Mill, about a mile from Olney. Cowper made a Latin translation of this poem, which he also sent to the *Gentleman's Magazine*. See *To Unwin*, February 7, 1785.

I

NOTES.

2. **colonnade** (from Ital. *colonna*, Lat. *columna*, a column) is strictly 'a row of columns.' It is here applied to the plantation of poplars with their straight column-like trunks.

4. **his.** See note, p. 106, l. 4.

5. **Twelve years.** Cowper removed to Olney on September 14, 1767; so that either he did not visit his "favourite field" till five years later, in 1772 (see Introduction), which seems unlikely, or he wrote this poem in or about the year 1779, and kept it by him till the publication of his first volume had given him a poetical standing, and he began to send pieces to the *Gentleman's Magazine*.

15. The line pictures the grassy grave-mound with its headstone in the churchyard.

16. **Ere another,** etc. Fresh trees have sprung up in Lynch Close since the poet's day.

19. **life be a dream.** A common comparison; cf. Bible, *Job*, xx. 8 : "He (man) shall fly away as a *dream*"; and Shaks. *Tempest*, IV. i. 156-158 :

> "We are such stuff
> As *dreams* are made on, and our little life
> Is rounded with a sleep."

And cf. *The Valediction*, 44.

THE ROSE.

INTRODUCTION.

This "exquisite little piece," as St. Beuve calls it, was written in June, 1783, and first published in the *Gentleman's Magazine* for June, 1785, and afterwards in *Poems, 1794.* Cowper enclosed it in a letter to Unwin, June 8, 1783, in which he says : "On the other side I send you a something, a song if you please, composed last Thursday—the incident happened the day before." And in a subsequent letter to the same (February 7, 1785) he tells Unwin that he has sent to the *Gentleman's Magazine* a piece "on a Rose-bud, the neck of which I inadvertently broke." When first printed, with only Cowper's initials attached, a Mrs. C. foolishly claimed the song as her own. Thus in a letter to Lady Hesketh, January 8, 1787, Cowper writes : "The Rose in question was a rose given to Lady Austen by Mrs. Unwin, and the incident that suggested the subject occurred in the room in which you slept at the vicarage, which

Lady Austen made her dining-room. Some time since, Mr. Bull going to London, I gave him a copy of it, which he undertook to convey to Nichols, the printer of the Gentleman's Magazine. He showed it to a Mrs. C——, who begged to copy it, and promised to send it to the printer's by her servant. Three or four months afterwards, and when I had concluded it was lost, I saw it in the Gentleman's Magazine with my signature, W. C. Poor simpleton ! she will find now perhaps that the Rose had a thorn, and that she has pricked her fingers with it." This last remark is explained by a subsequent letter to Lady Throckmorton, April 16, 1792, in which he says : " A lady in London stole my song on the broken Rose, or rather would have stolen, and have passed it for her own. But she too was unfortunate in her attempt ; for there happened to be a female cousin of mine (*i.e.* Lady Hesketh) in company, who knew that I had written it."

NOTES.

2. **Mary to Anna.** Mary is Mrs. Unwin, and Anna is Lady Austen ; see Introduction.

10. **nosegay**, lit. a *gay* or pretty thing for the *nose*, *i.e.* to smell ; and so a bunch of flowers, a bouquet.

14. **by**, in regard to, towards ; as in "Do as you would be done *by*."

19. **And the tear**, etc. Canon Benham thinks that Sir J. Stephen was undoubtedly right in regarding the "moral" of this poem as a gentle rebuke to Newton, "whose ungentle touch was occasionally put forth at the vicarage to dry up his tears."

address, skill, adroitness.

MRS. THROCKMORTON'S BULLFINCH.

INTRODUCTION.

This poem was first published in *Poems*, 1794. In a letter to Samuel Rose, September 25, 1788, Cowper writes : " Weston has not been without its tragedies since you left us ; Mrs. Throckmorton's piping bullfinch has been eaten by a rat, and the villain left nothing but poor Bully's beak behind him. It will be a wonder if this event does not at some convenient time employ my versifying passion. Did ever fair lady, from the Lesbia of Catullus to the present day, lose her bird and find no poet to commemorate the loss ?"

Maria Throckmorton was the wife of Mr. (afterwards Sir) John Courtenay Throckmorton. The poet in his letters playfully calls them Mr. and Mrs. Frog. They resided at Weston Hall, in Weston Underwood, a mile from Olney. They were Roman Catholics, but Cowper became very intimate with them, and to her is addressed his poem, *The Wish,* or *The Poet's New Year's Gift,* written for January 1, 1788.

NOTES.

1. **Ye Nymphs,** *i.e.* ladies such as Lesbia, the death of whose pet sparrow was sung by the Roman poet Catullus. *Nymph,* in eighteenth century literature, was 'poetical' for *girl* or *maiden,* as *swain,* a peasant, was used for *young man* or *lover.* Cf. *Task,* iii. 316-318:

> " How many self-deluded nymphs and swains,
>   Who dream they have a taste for fields and groves,
>   Would find them hideous nurseries of the spleen ! "

Also cf. *The Dog and the Water-lily,* 7, and note.

If e'er your eyes were red. Cf. Catullus's lyric, 16-18:

> *Io miselle passer,*
> *Tua nunc opera meae puellae*
> *Flendo turgiduli rubent ocelli.*

' Alas, poor little sparrow, it is your doing that now my lady's eyes are red and swollen with weeping.'

4, 6. Her favourite...(being) **Assassined,** an absolute construction.

5. What will not ... rage ? *Do* is understood after "rage." This seems to be a reminiscence of Vergil, *Aen.* iii. 56, 57: *Quid non mortalia pectora cogis, Auri sacra fames ?"* ' What dost thou not drive men to, cursed hunger for gold ?'

6. Assassined, by poetic license for the more common "assassinated." *Assassin* (from the Arabic *hashish,* a decoction of hemp) = *Haschischin,* the drinkers of this intoxicating beverage, a well-known sect in Palestine who flourished in the thirteenth century under the Sheik Haschischin, who roused his followers' spirits by help of this drink, and sent them to stab his enemies, especially the leading Crusaders.

7. Rhenus, the Latin name for the river Rhine.

8. sprung. See note, p. 83, l. 60.

12. flageolet...flute. These are the same word, both being derived from O.Fr. *flageoler,* Castrais *flaguta,* Lang. *flauta.*

13. The honours ... poll, ' the beauty or charm of his black head,' or ' his beautiful black head.' *Honours* here is an imitation of the Latin, like Horace's *ruris honores,* ' the beautiful country.' *Poll* is especially the back part of the head.

13. **ebon**, adjective from noun *ebony*, a hard, black wood. Milton (*L'Allegro*, 8) has "*ebon* shades."

15. **the hue**, etc., *i.e.* vermilion.

16. **Aurora**, the early morning. *Aurora* was the Roman goddess of the dawn.

17. **When piping winds**, etc. Cf. Tennyson, *Maud*, Part I., xxii. 2, "A breeze of morning moves." Rogers (*Epitaph on a Robin-Redbreast*, 2) has the expression "piping winds."

24. **latticed**, furnished with a network of crossed rods. *Lattice* = *lattis*, *lath*-work.

25. **the grate**, the frame-work. *Grate* is from Lat. *crates*, 'a hurdle.'

27. **plumage sake**. *Plumage* is in the possessive case. For ease of pronunciation the *s* of the possessive was, and is, often omitted before the word *sake*, as in 'for *mercy* sake.' But "*humour's* sake," *Epitaph on a Hare*, 33. Sometimes the apostrophe was also dropt, as here, and in *Task*, iv. 665, "For *interest* sake." Similarly Milton (*Par. Lost*, xi. 514) has "For his Maker's *image* sake," and Shakspere (1 *Henry IV.* v. i. 65) has "For *safety* sake." Cf. "*Hebrus'* side," below, l. 63.

28. **wands.** A *wand* is lit. what can be *wound* into wicker-work, a little twig, and so happens to be a very appropriate word here.

30. **swains**, 'poetical' for *peasants* ; cf. *Heroism*, 39.

31. **Night veiled the pole.** This expression, like "honours," above (l. 13), is an imitation of the Latin ; cf. Vergil's *Nox atra polum ... tenebat*, 'Black night possessed the pole' (*Aen.* v. 721). The introduction of these classical phrases gives a happy mock-heroic cast to the poem.

33. **Subsistence to provide**, *i.e.* to provide himself with subsistence or food.

34. **on the scout**, on the look-out : cf. *The Cricket*, 11. *Scout*, here used as an abstract noun, is from O. Fr. *escoute*, 'a spy,' from *escouter*, Lat. *auscultare*, ' to hearken.'

36. **badger-coloured**, brownish-gray. The badger gets its name from the notion that this animal lays up a store of grain ; for *badger* = *bladger* = O. Fr. *bladier* = Low Lat. *bladarius*, 'a corn-dealer.' The Low Lat. *bladum*, 'corn,' is a contraction of *abladum*, *ablatum*, 'corn that has been *carried* or gathered in.'

38. **'gan.** See note, p. 103, l. 44.

39. **something in the wind**, etc. He thought he smelt something in the air that was better than all the books, etc.

43. **by adverse fate impressed**, *i.e.* the calamity that was about to befall him produced the dream. *Impressed* agrees with *dream*.

50. **Right to his mark,** straight to his object.

51. **Ah, Muse!** etc., *i.e.* the details are too horrible to be described in verse. There were nine Muses, goddesses who presided over all the liberal arts, but especially poetry.

51, 52. **to speak Minutely,** to tell minutely or in detail.

55. In the earlier editions this line stood thus:

> " He left it—but he should have ta'en,"

with "strain" in the next line instead of "lay." *Oh, had he* = ' Oh, (I) would that he had.'

57. **mellifluous,** lit. flowing with honey; honey-dropping, honey-sweet.

58. **repaid him well,** ' fitly punished him '; ' paid him out,' as we say.

I wote, I think, in my opinion. *Wot* (Cowper writes it "wote" to rhyme with "throat") is the present indicative of the infinitive *wit*, O.E. *witan,* to know, seen in *wittingly,* ' knowingly.' The past tense is *wist.*

60. **Fast stuck,** *i.e.* by being fast stuck; "stuck" agrees with "beak," and "his own" with "throat" understood.

61. **the Muses.** See note to l. 51 above.

62. **So, when,** etc. Orpheus, son of the Muse Calliope, played so sweetly on the lyre that mountains and trees and savage things followed obedient to his melody. His coldness offended the Thracian women (the "Bacchanalians"), who attacked him while they celebrated the orgies of the wine-god Bacchus (the *Bacchanalia*), and, after tearing his body in pieces, threw his head into the river Hebrus, in Thrace, by which it was carried down into the Aegean sea. Cf. Milton, *Lycidas,* 58-63:

> " What could the Muse herself (have done) that Orpheus bore,
> The Muse herself, for her enchanting son
> Whom universal Nature did lament ;
> When by the rout that made the hideous roar,
> His gory visage down the stream was sent,
> Down the swift Hebrus to the Lesbian shore ? "

63. **Hebrus' side.** See note to l. 27 above.

64. **tree-enchanter.** Cf. Shakspere's song :

> "Orpheus with his lute made trees,
> And the mountain tops that freeze,
>   Bow themselves, when he did sing."

And *Merchant of Venice,* v. i. 879, 880:

> " The poet
> Did feign that Orpheus drew trees, stones, and floods."

ODE TO APOLLO.

INTRODUCTION.

This poem was first published in *Poems*, 1794. It was composed some time before December 19, 1787, since in a letter of that date to Lady Hesketh, Cowper writes: "I received also a letter from Anonymous ... in which letter allusion is made to a certain piece by me composed, entitled, I believe, the Drop of Ink. The only copy I ever gave of that piece I gave to yourself. It is *possible*, therefore, that between you and Anonymous there may be some communication."

NOTES.

1. **Patron**, etc. Phoebus Apollo was not only the sun-god, but also the god of music and poetry. Hence Cowper addresses him under both designations, and rallies him for drying up the ink of one of his own henchmen (ll. 9-12). He figures as a tall, handsome young man, holding in his hand a bow, and sometimes a lyre.

those luckless brains, *i.e.* the poets. Cowper writes in a bantering vein.

2. **to the wrong side leaning**, taking the wrong course, acting perversely.

7. **Pay tribute**, etc. Since their waters are constantly being evaporated by the sun's heat.

9. **the noon of day**, the mid-day sky.

15. **dense and rare**, *i.e.* where the atmosphere is dense or rarefied. Cf. the quotation from Milton in note, p. 90, l. 40.

18. **millions**, *i.e.* of vapours.

19. **an Iris**, a rainbow. Iris, the messenger of the gods, represented the rainbow in Greek and Roman mythology.

24. **to be forgot**. The poet modestly intimates that all the ink that he has hitherto used has been wasted, except this drop; though he allows himself in the last two lines an aspiration that something better may happen to the remainder.

26. **thy bow**. See note to l. 1 above. Cowper here identifies the legendary bow of Apollo with the rainbow.

THE FAITHFUL BIRD.

INTRODUCTION.

This poem was first published in *Poems*, 1794. In a letter to Unwin, August 4, 1783, Cowper writes: "I have two goldfinches, which in summer occupy the greenhouse. A few days since, being employed in cleaning out their cages, I placed that which I had in my hand upon the table, while the other hung against the wall ; the windows and the doors stood wide open. I went to fill the fountain at the pump, and on my return was not a little surprised to find a goldfinch sitting on the top of the cage I had been cleaning, and singing to and kissing the goldfinch within. I approached him, and he discovered no fear ; still nearer, and he discovered none. I advanced my hand towards him, and he took no notice of it. I seized him and supposed I had caught a new bird, but casting my eye on the other cage perceived my mistake. Its inhabitant, during my absence, had contrived to find an opening, where the wire had been a little bent, and made no other use of the escape it afforded him than to salute his friend, and to converse with him more intimately than he had done before. I restored him to his proper mansion, but in vain. In less than a minute he had thrust his little person through the aperture again, and again perched upon his neighbour's cage, kissing him, as at the first, and singing, as if transported with the fortunate adventure. I could not but respect such friendship, as for the sake of its gratification had twice declined an opportunity to be free, and, consenting to their union, resolved that for the future one cage should hold them both."

NOTES.

1. The Greenhouse. The poet's greenhouse, which was of his own building, is frequently referred to in his Letters. In the extremely hot summer of 1781 he tells Newton (August 16) that he had "converted it into a summer parlour. The walls hung with garden mats, and the floor covered with a carpet, the sun, too, in a great measure excluded by an awning of mats ... it affords us by far the pleasantest retreat in Olney." Again, *To Unwin*, June 8, 1783 : "Our severest winter, commonly called the spring, is now over, and I find myself seated in my favourite recess, the greenhouse." Many of his letters are dated from this favourite retreat.

2. My shrubs displaced. Cf. *To Lady Hesketh*, February 9, 1786 : "My dear, I will not let you come till the end of May, or beginning of June, because before that time my greenhouse will not be ready to receive us, and it is the only pleasant room belonging to us. When the plants go out, we go in."

9. list, desire, choose. The verb is formed by regular vowel-change from the O.E. noun *lust*, pleasure. Thus *listless* means ' devoid of desire,' and so 'careless.'

14. With force ... suppressed. Cf. the Latin proverb (Horace, *Ep.* I. x. 24) : *Naturam expellas furca, tamen usque recurret,*

'Though you forcibly (lit. with a pitchfork) drive out Nature, she will still resume her sway.' For this line editions 1794 to 1806 read : "Instinct is never quite suppressed."

16. The same editions have "which" instead of "that" in this line.

25. So settling, etc. This stanza in the above editions stood thus :

> " For settling on his grated roof,
>   He chirp'd and kiss'd him, giving proof
>   That he desired no more ;
>   Nor would forsake his cage at last,
>   Till gently seiz'd, I shut him fast,
>   A prisoner as before."

28. stand, standing-place. Cf. "standing," *The Needless Alarm*, 120.

31. taste. The old editions read "knew."

33. Fandango, a lively Spanish dance, in which the dancers carry castanets.

rout, in its secondary sense of a 'crowd,' was a common expression in Cowper's day for an evening party, the modern 'At Home.' Cf. *Task*, ii. 629, etc. :

> "The *Rout* is Folly's circle .   .   .
>   .   .   .   .   .   She that asks
> Her dear five hundred friends, contemns them all,
> And hates their coming."

And *The Jackdaw*, 26.

THE NEEDLESS ALARM.

INTRODUCTION.

This poem was first published in *Poems*, 1794. It is written in Cowper's best style, with a delightful humour and gentle satire that is peculiarly his. The whole scene is depicted for us as by one who had himself observed it and noted every detail. We know from his letter to Lady Hesketh, March 3, 1788, that he had once been in at the death of a fox.

NOTES.

3. Kilwick's. Kilwick and Dinglederry (l. 36) were two woods belonging to Mr. John Throckmorton, Cowper's friend and neighbour at Weston Underwood. For *echoing*, cf. l. 35.

4. bitch-fox, rather than *vixen*, is the term employed by sportsmen ; with masculine *dog-fox*.

hapless. Because her young were preserved only to be hunted ; see the next two lines.

7. Contusion ... spine, running the risk of breaking his neck or his back (by a fall from his horse). Cowper condemned "sport" as cruel : the "sportsman" and "the folly of his life's mad scene" is included in *Progress of Error*, 82-95, where he

> "Leaps every fence but one, there falls and dies."

And in the *Task* he calls hunting

> "Detested sport,
> That owes its pleasures to another's pain."

See the whole passage, Bk. iii., 306-336. Cf. also ll. 26-28 below.

10. a bottom, a valley, a hollow.

11. had once a head, had leaves on top. Cf. Ben Jonson :

> "The balmy west wind blows, and every sense
> Is soothed and courted :—trees *have got their heads*,
> The fields their coats."

12. oven-wood, dead wood fit only for burning.

13. watery bourn, the brook that bounds it. *Bourn* is a doublet of *bound*, a boundary, limit.

16. horrid, used in its Latin meaning of 'rough, bristling.' So Milton, *Par. Lost*, i. 563, 564 :

> "They stand, a *horrid* front
> Of dreadful length and dazzling arms."

And *Ibid.* ii. 710 : "His (the comet's) *horrid* hair."

18. For baking ... lime, to get earth for baking into bricks, or limestone for burning into lime.

20. fieldfare, lit. 'field-wanderer, traverser of the field,' is a bird of the Thrush family.

wintry guest. It is a winter resident in Great Britain, coming from the far north, where it breeds.

24. Now therefore. Because the crops, being gathered, could not be injured by huntsmen and hounds.

26. a whole gamut, etc. Shakspere, in this respect, had a very different ear from Cowper's ; cf. *A Midsummer-Night's Dream*, iv. i. 120-123, where Theseus describes his hounds as

> "Match'd in mouth like bells,
> Each under each. A cry more tuneable
> Was never holla'd to, nor cheer'd with horn,"

in which 'each under each,' *i.e.* forming a musical scale, well illustrates Cowper's 'gamut.' This word is made up of O.F.

game, Gk. *gamma*, the letter *g* (which is the last of the series of letters used to represent the seven notes of the scale, and which gave its name to the whole), and Lat. *ut*, the old name for the first note in singing, now called *do*.   *Heavenly* is ironical.

30. **His lamp**, etc., *i.e.* it was now mid-day.

33, 34. **Ere yet ... found.**   As soon as hounds discover a scent, they give tongue.

41, 42. **conveyed ... spread.**   For the rhyme, cf. note, p. 65, ll. 1, 3.

42. **kind contagion.**   Contagion, being generally used of disease, is here modified by "kind."   Their peace was *pleasantly* "catching."

44. **'Gan.**   The apostrophe should be omitted, since the verb *gin* is not a contraction of *begin*, but the original word whence *begin* is formed.   Cf. notes, p. 97, l. 38 ; p. 132, l. 92.

45. **crash**, which is an imitative word, allied to *craze*, *crush*, and *crack*, expresses, to Cowper's ear, by the suddenness and harshness it implies, the baying of the hounds.

47-54. **The sheep recumbent**, etc.   Note the accuracy of this description, one of many that justify Cowper's claim that his "descriptions are all from nature ; not one of them second-handed" (*To Unwin*, Oct. 10, 1784).

48. **phalanx**, close array, serried ranks.

49. **Admiring**, in its Latin meaning of 'wondering at.'   So Milton, *Par. Lost*, i. 690, "Let none *admire* That riches grow in Hell" ; ii. 677, "The undaunted Fiend what this might be *admir'd*, Admir'd, not fear'd."   Cf. note, p. 137, l. 1.

50. The Alexandrine line (see p. 116), with its extra foot, well expresses the repeated circuits of the animals.

52. **That flight**, etc., that they made no forward progress by running round and round.   *Nought* is an adverb.

60. **He hears**, etc.   See General Introduction, p. xxiv., and cf. Wordsworth, *Lines written in early Spring*, 11, 12 :

> "And 'tis my faith that every flower
> Enjoys the air it breathes."

63. **nicer still,** still more exact or delicate.   Cf. notes, p. 68, l. 8 ; p. 126, l. 24.

68. **articulation**, clear expression ; lit. 'division into joints,' the joints of speech being words and syllables ; Lat. *articulus*, dim. of *artus*, a joint, a limb.

70. **glossary**, dictionary of hard words ; Lat. *glossa*, a hard word needing explanation.

71. **This truth,** etc., it was necessary to state this fact beforehand as a motto or introduction to what follows.

75. **periwigs.** *Periwig* (of which *wig* is a curtailed form) = *perwigge* = *perwicke*, from Old Dutch *peruyk*, a peruke. Periwigs were commonly worn in Cowper's day, and the fashion prevailed in England more or less till about 1810.

80. For science and mathematics, included under the term "philosophy," Cowper had little taste or admiration. Cf. General Introduction, p. xvii.

81. **a mutton,** a sheep. The poet playfully uses the word in its old meaning ; Fr. *mouton*, a sheep.

86. **womb.** Cf. *Heroism*, 12.

87. **prison-house.** A Shaksperian word ; see *Hamlet*, I. v. 14.

91. **what time,** at the time when. *Time* is to be parsed as an adverbial objective.

93. **that tremendous bray alone,** *i.e.* the sound of the huntsman's horn without the baying of the hounds.

100. **That owns a carcass,** that inhabits a body.

106. **Cambrian,** Welsh, Cambria being the ancient name for Wales, or land of the Cimbri, a Celtic race. Wales is famous for its breed of sheep.

107, 108. **How! leap,** etc. Cf. Martial, *Epp.* ii. 80 (of one who killed himself when defeated in battle): *Non furor est ne moriare mori?* 'Is it not madness to die that you may escape death?'

113, 114. Clothed as we are in wool, we should be inextricably entangled in the brambles.

115. **Dapple's.** *Dapple* is a name for an ass, in allusion to the gray spot (*dapple*) or mark on its back.

120. **standing,** standing-place, location. So "stand," *The Faithful Bird*, 28.

124. **Reynard** is the name of the fox in the famous Teutonic epic, *Reincke Fuchs*, "The History of Reynard the Fox." The word means 'strong in counsel.'

131. **So sweet.** Cf. l. 8. The "huntsman" is the man who has charge of the pack of hounds and who blows the horn.

133. **Live till to-morrow,** if you live or wait till to-morrow. *Live* is an imperative used to express a supposition ; cf. note, p. 75, l. 10 ; and Tennyson, *Lancelot and Elaine*, 1064 :

> "*Give* me good fortune, I will strike him dead."

THE DOG AND THE WATER-LILY.

INTRODUCTION.

This poem was sent to Lady Hesketh with a letter dated August 21, 1788, and was first printed in a separate form, with the *Lines on the Receipt of my Mother's Picture*, price 6d., pp. 14, in 1798; and included in *Poems*, 1798. Cowper tells the story in a letter to Lady Hesketh, June 27, 1788: "I must tell you a feat of my dog Beau. Walking by the river side I observed some water-lilies floating at a little distance from the bank. They are a large white flower, with an orange-coloured eye, very beautiful. I had a desire to gather one, and, having your long cane in my hand, by the help of it endeavoured to bring one of them within my reach; but the attempt proved vain, and I walked forward. Beau had all the while observed me very attentively. Returning soon after toward the same place, I observed him plunge into the river, while I was about forty yards distant from him, and, when I had nearly reached the spot, he swam to land with a lily in his mouth, which he came and laid at my foot." He remarks in his next letter of July 5: "Beau's performance was exactly such as I represented it, without any embellishment. I may now add that the next time we walked to the same place together he repeated it." The incident occurred near Goosey Bridge, close to Olney. In another letter to Samuel Rose, August 18, 1788, Cowper writes: "I have not been idle since you went, having not only laboured as usual at the *Iliad*, but composed a *spick and span* new piece, called ' The Dog and the Water-Lily,' which you shall see when we meet again." Yet another letter to Lady Hesketh, December 13, 1789, ends with the following paragraph: "Received from my master, on account current with Lady Hesketh, the sum of—one kiss on my forehead. Witness my paw, Beau × his mark."

The poet draws two moral lessons from the incident: (1) a lesson for mankind, teaching them to display greater kindness and love towards one another, since even a dog can show himself superior to them in this respect; (2) a lesson for himself, of love and gratitude to God, the All-Giver, since the dog showed such love to his master who provided for his wants.

NOTES.

1. **airs**, poetical for ' breezes.' Generally the plural *airs* means conceited behaviour, as in ' He gave himself airs.'

2. **Ouse's**. The Ouse, "slow winding through a level plain"[1] (hence "silent," l. 2), the river on which Olney stands, has been made famous by Cowper's poetry, as the Thames by Pope, or the

---

[1] *Task*, l. 163.

Duddon by Wordsworth. The Ouse is personified here (cf. "his,' l. 4) and so has no article before it.

3. 'scaped, for *escaped*. Cf. Shaks. *Merchant of Venice*, II. ii. 148, 150 : "To *'scape* drowning thrice ... here are simple *scapes*." Milton has the verb *scape* frequently and the noun *scape* once (*Par. Reg.* ii. 189) ; and cf. *scapegoat, scapegrace.*

literary cares. Cowper was at this time engaged upon his translation of Homer.

4. his. The poets make rivers, winds, and mountains masculine ; cf. *The Poplar Field*, 4.

5. My spaniel. On the death of two of his hares and the decrepitude of the third, Puss, through old age, the poet provided himself with a dog called Mungo. Mungo was succeeded by another dog, Marquis, and he again by Cowper's favourite, Beau. Beau had been procured for him towards the end of 1787 by two young ladies (the "two nymphs" of l. 7), Charlotte and Barbara, the daughters of Sir Robert Gunning, of Horton, near Olney. They were grand-daughters of a brother of the celebrated beauties of the reigns of George II. and III. We first hear of Beau in a letter to Lady Hesketh, December 19, 1787, where he is spoken of as "unrivalled in personal endowments by any dog in this country." Another letter to the same, July 5, 1788, tells us that "he is regularly combed, and his ears, which are remarkably handsome, are my own peculiar care. They gather burrs while he treads all the thickets in his way, from which I deliver them myself as soon as we get home. But, having taught him to take the water, and even to delight in it, I never give him a forced washing, lest he should contract a hydrophobia, and refuse the river." For Cowper's fondness for animals see General Introduction, pp. xix., xx. He has two other poems relating to Beau. *Spaniel*, a dog of Spanish breed, is from the Span. *español*, 'Spanish.'

6. high in pedigree, of good breed.

7. Two nymphs, etc. The prose order is 'Two nymphs adorned etc., found that spaniel for me.' See note to l. 5 above. *Nymphs* is 'poetical' for *young ladies*; see note, p. 96, l. 1 ; and *The Retired Cat*, 18.

9. wantoned, frolicked. This is the adjective *wanton* (= O.E. *wan-towen*, un-educated, un-restrained) used as a verb. Cf. *The Retired Cat*, 32.

flags. *Flag*, the water-plant, and *flag*, an ensign, are from the same root as *flag*, to droop, because they both wave or flutter in the wind.

12. scarce, for *scarcely*. So "intent" (l. 15) for *intently*, "impatient" (l. 34) for *impatiently*, and "chief" (l. 41) for *chiefly*.

17, 18. **I sought To steer it,** I tried to guide or push it with the stick, so as to bring it close to land.

19. **still,** continually, at each attempt.

21. **Beau** is French for 'beautiful.'

pains, 'trouble,' 'efforts,' as in 'to take pains.'

22. **With fixed,** etc., with steadfast, thoughtful look.

25. **cherup,** a shrill cry or whistle, is the same word as *chirrup,* a lengthened form of *chirp,* a word imitative of the sound. It is used as a verb in *Task,* iii. 9 :

"He *cherups* brisk his ear-erecting steed."

26. **his dream,** his musing state, his reverie.

29. **My ramble** (being) **ended,** an absolute clause.

ended. Editions 1798 to 1806 have "finished," for which "ended" was substituted in all subsequent editions.

31. **wreath,** the cluster of water-lilies.

39, 40. **My dog,** etc., my dog's loving intelligence shall put to shame the boasted superiority of man over the brute creation. When men hear the story of what my dog has done they will feel ashamed that a dog should show greater gratitude and affection than a man. *Mortify* is lit. 'to make dead,' Lat. *morti,* death, and *fic-* (*fac-ere*), to cause ; hence, to subdue, humiliate.

40. **superior breed,** higher order or rank in the scale of creation. The dog belongs to the order *Carnivora,* the 9th order ; man to the order *Primates,* the 13th or highest order.

41, 43. **enjoin ... thine.** For the rhyme see note, p. 65, ll.1, 3.

42. **Awake at duty's call,** obedient to the claims of duty.

44. **Him,** *i e.* God.

ON THE RECEIPT OF MY MOTHER'S PICTURE.

INTRODUCTION.

This poem was written between February 27 and March 12, 1790. It was printed in a separate form with *The Dog and the Water-Lily,* price 6d., pp. 14, in 1798 ; and included in *Poems,* 1798.

Ann Bodham was the third daughter of the Rev. Roger Donne, Rector of Catfield, Norfolk, who was brother to Cowper's mother. She was therefore the poet's first cousin and was his playfellow in childhood—an intercourse which she renewed by sending him his mother's picture, which she did at the instance of John Johnson, her nephew (*To J. Johnson,* Feb. 28, 1790). She had married the Rev. Thomas Bodham in 1771.

In a letter to her, dated Weston, February 27, 1790, acknow-
ledging the receipt of the picture, Cowper writes: "The world
could not have furnished you with a present so acceptable to me
as the picture which you have so kindly sent me. I received it
the night before last, and viewed it with a trepidation of nerves
and spirits somewhat akin to what I should have felt had the
dear original presented herself to my embraces. I kissed it, and
hung it where it is the last that I see at night, and of course the
first on which I open my eyes in the morning. She died when I
had completed my sixth year ; yet I remember her well, and am
an ocular witness of the great fidelity of the copy. I remember
too a multitude of the maternal tendernesses which I received
from her, and which have endeared her memory to me beyond
expression."

In a letter to Lady Hesketh, February 26, 1790, he writes :
"I am delighted with Mrs. Bodham's kindness in giving me the
only picture of my mother to be found, I suppose, in all the
world ; I had rather possess it than the richest jewel in the
British crown, for I loved her with an affection that her death,
fifty-two years since, has not in the least abated .... Everybody
loved her, and with an amiable character so impressed upon all
her features, everybody was sure to do so."

Again, in a letter to John Johnson, February 28, 1790,
he remarks : "I am perhaps the only person living who re-
members her ; but I remember her well, and can attest on my
own knowledge the truth of the resemblance. Amiable and
elegant as the countenance is, such exactly was her own; she
was one of the tenderest parents, and so just a copy of her is
therefore to me invaluable."

Once more, in a letter to Mrs. King, March 12, 1790, he says :
"I have lately received from a female cousin of mine in Norfolk,
whom I have not seen these thirty years, a picture of my own
mother. She died when I wanted two days of being six years
old ; yet I remember her perfectly, find the picture a strong
likeness of her, and because her memory has been ever precious
to me, have written a poem on the receipt of it ; a poem which,
one excepted, I had more pleasure in writing than any that I
ever wrote. That one was addressed to a lady whom I expect in
a few minutes to come down to breakfast, and who has supplied
to me the place of my own mother—my own invaluable mother,
these six-and-twenty years." The excepted poem must be the
sonnet *To Mrs. Unwin* ; see the Introduction to that piece, p. 133.

These are some of the most pathetic verses in the English
language. "I wrote them," writes Cowper (*To Lady Hesketh*,
April 30, 1790), "not without tears, therefore I presume it may
be that they are felt by others." "As we read them," remarks
St. Beuve, "we find not only the affectionate emotion which
would be in the heart of many sons at the contemplation of that

which recalls happy years to them, but we also recognise there the specially pathetic, tenderly sensitive and sorrowful part of that nature of Cowper's, which required beyond everything the warmth and shelter of the domestic nest."

The picture, painted in oils by Heines, represents Mrs. Cowper to waist, miniature size, full face, low blue dress, on canvas 6 × 5 inches. It is now in the possession of the Rev. C. E. Donne, Vicar of Faversham, Kent, The poet's mother is buried within the altar-rails of Berkhampstead Church, where, on the south wall is a tablet to her memory, commencing—

> " Consigned to Earth lies (young bereft of life)
> The best of Mothers and the kindest Wife."

NOTES.

1. **Oh that.** The interjection expresses an aspiration, so that 'oh that' is equivalent to 'I wish that.'

those lips. Cowper is, as it were, addressing the picture.

3. **are thine,** *i.e.* the picture is a faithful likeness; see Introduction.

smile. The first and subsequent editions to 1806 had "smiles." In edition 1808 it was altered to "smile."

5. **distinct,** for *distinctly*, like 'slow' for *slowly* in l. 29, and 'light' for *lightly* in l. 95.

7. **intelligence.** Shakspere (*Macbeth*, III. iv. 95) uses 'speculation' in this sense (of the ghost):

> "Thou hast no *speculation* in those eyes
> Which thou dost glare with !"

8. **the art,** *i.e.* the art of painting.

9. **baffles,** foils. 'To baffle' originally meant 'to disgrace,' being applied to the regular process by which an openly perjured man was held up to public contempt.

10. **it,** *i.e.* the intelligence. Time, through death, would quench the look of intelligence, were it not that the art of painting fixes it on the canvas.

11. **remembrancer,** that which brings to the remembrance; reminder.

16. **as the precept were her own,** in the way in which (I should obey), were the precept her own ; as if she bade me herself. Cf. *John Gilpin*, 128. In this old use of *as*, the *if* is not understood, but is implied in the subjunctive mood (Abbott, *Shaks. Gr.* §107). Cf. Shaks. *Macbeth*, I. iv. 11 :

> " To throw away the dearest thing he owed,
> *As* 'twere a careless trifle."

.   K

19. **Elysian reverie,** a blessed or heavenly waking dream. Elysium or the Elysian fields was the Greek Heaven, the abode of the blest. Similarly Cowper (*Retirement*, 199) speaks of Nature's "Elysian scenes."

24. **Wretch,** wretched, unhappy. The latter half of the verse is an absolute clause.

25. **unfelt.** The editions 1798 to 1806 had "unseen."

29. **hearse** is from the Lat. *hirpicem*, a harrow, and was applied to (1) a triangular frame for supporting lights, so called from its resemblance to a harrow, and used at funerals; hence to (2) a funeral pageant; (3) a frame on which a corpse was laid, or the tomb itself; (4) a carriage in which the dead are carried to the grave (as here).

31. **wept a last adieu.** *Adieu* is to be parsed as a partially cognate object of the verb *wept*. It is not cognate in form, and is only partially cognate in meaning, since it contains a descriptive sense of its own in addition to its cognate meaning. Thus 'to weep an *adieu*' means 'to weep a *weeping of adieu*,' 'to weep farewell tears.' See note, p. 75, l. 14. *Adieu* = Fr. *à Dieu*, (I commit you) to God = God be with you = good-bye.

33. **Adieus.** Observe the English plural, *adieus*, instead of the French, *adieux*. Similarly Pope (*Rape of the Lock*, 653) has *beaus*.

34. **May I** = if I may; cf. l. 81 below, and note, p. 69, l. 17.   '

35. **The parting word,** the word used at parting, viz., farewell. Editions 1798 to 1808 have "sound" for "word." *Parting* is not a participle, but a verbal noun.

36. **maidens,** maid-servants. *Themselves* is in apposition with "maidens."

38. **What ardently,** etc. Cf. Shaks. 2 *Henry IV.* iv. v. 92:
  "Thy wish was father, Harry, to that thought."
And Caesar, *Bell. Gall.* iii. 18: *Fere libenter homines quod volunt credunt,* 'Commonly what men wish they willingly believe.'   .

40. **expectation.** Editions 1798 to 1808 have "disappointment."

41. **Dupe of to-morrow,** deceived in my hopes of future happiness. Cf. l. 24 above, and Dryden, *Aurengzebe*, iv. 1:
  "When I consider life, 'tis all a cheat,
    Yet, fooled with hope, men favour the deceit;
    Trust on, and think to-morrow will repay:
    To-morrow's falser than the former day;

Lies worse ; and while it says we shall be blest
With some new joys, cuts off what we possest.
Strange cozenage ! none would live past years again,
Yet all hope pleasure in what yet remain."

Similarly Tibullus, *Carm.* vi. 19, 20 : *Credula vitam Spes fovet, et melius cras fore semper ait,* 'Hope by its credulity fosters life, and is always telling us that to-morrow will be better.'

48. **Robin.** His full name was Robert Pope. He died in 1767.

49. **Drew me.** Robin pulled the little cart in which he rode to school.

50. **bauble coach,** toy or miniature coach. This *bauble* is from Ital. *babbola,* child's toys, from *babbeo,* a simpleton, a *babbler,* one who says 'ba, ba.'

51. **velvet-capped,** wearing a velvet cap.

53. **the pastoral house,** the rectory at Great Berkhampstead ; see General Introduction, p. ix. The house was pulled down some thirty-seven years ago, and a new rectory built. *Pastoral* means here 'occupied by the pastor or clergyman.'

54. **Short-lived possession.** Cowper's father died July, 1756, at the age of sixty-one. He married a second time after the death of the poet's mother.

55. **That memory keeps.** Forty-seven years after her death Cowper writes to Hill, November 1784 : "I can truly say that not a week passes (perhaps I might with equal veracity say a day) in which I do not think of her. Such was the impression her tenderness made upon me, though the opportunity she had for showing it was so short."

56. **a storm,** the shocks and turmoil of human existence which make us lose memory of past events.

58. **nightly visits,** visits paid every night. *Nightly* in poetry often means 'nocturnal,' as in *Task,* iv. 432 : "the *nightly* thief."

59. **know me ... laid,** see that I was safe and warmly covered up in bed.

61. **confectionary,** preserved, candied ; lit. 'made up,' Lat. *confectus, conficere,* to put together. The noun is *confectionery ;* cf. *stationary* (adj.) and *stationery* (noun).

62. **waters,** a poetical plural, like *snows* in *Task,* iv. 123.

63. **they shone.** Similarly Shakspere's schoolboy in *As You Like It,* ii. vii. 146, creeps to school "with *shining* morning face."

65. **Thy constant flow,** etc. Cowper compares his mother's love to a stream flowing over level ground with even and continuous current ; whereas a love that is liable to fitful change

and caprice ("humour") is like a stream flowing over broken ground, disturbed by little falls and cataracts.

70. **Adds joy to duty**, makes the duty (of writing this poem) a pleasure.

71. **numbers** (Lat. *numeri*, verses; *numerus*, musical measure), for poetry or poetic rhythm, was a common 'poetical' word in Pope's time, who wrote of himself:

"I lisp'd in numbers, for the numbers came."

Cf. *Strada's Nightingale*, 4.

74. **his flight reversed**, an absolute clause; l. 89 contains two more such, and l. 103 has three; cf. Tennyson, *Recollections of the Arabian Nights*, 3:

"The tide of time flow'd back with me";

and Milton, *Nativity Ode*, xiv. :

"For, if such holy song
Enwrap our fancy long,
Time will run back and fetch the age of gold."

75. **tissued**, woven, embroidered.

77, **I pricked ... pin.** Placing a piece of paper on the under-side of the dress, he pricked round the edge of the pattern of the flower. Mr. Wright says : "In order to understand this, we must remember that a lady's dress in those days consisted, besides the gown proper, of a pair of folds reaching from the waist to the feet, and it was with these folds that children were wont to amuse themselves in the way related."

80. **days.** Editions 1798 to 1806 have "hours."

82. **I would not trust my heart.** *i.e.* with the opportunity of choosing ;—I am afraid my affection for my mother is so strong that it would not refuse the boon.

88-107. These lines are remarkable for their dignity and pathos. They are full of the inspiration that comes from genuine feeling. The metaphor is admirably preserved throughout, without being in the least degree forced. With them may be compared A. H. Clough's poem beginning "As ships, becalmed at eve, that lay," containing the same figure. Compare also Horace, *Odes*, i. 14; ii. 10. Cowper employs the same metaphor to illustrate his condition, in *To the Rev. Mr. Newton*, 13-16 :

"Your sea of troubles you have past,
And found the peaceful shore ;
I, tempest-tost, and wrecked at last,
Come home to port no more."

Also *The Castaway*, 61-66, and note, p. 135, l. 7.

88. **Albion's**, England's. The origin of the name seems to be doubtful. Milton says : "Sure enough we are that Britain hath

been anciently termed *Albion*, both by the Greeks and Romans."
It is probably derived from a Celtic word *alp, albin*, 'highlands,'
rather than from Lat. *albus*, 'white,' in allusion to the chalk
cliffs of its southern coast.

95. **streamers**, flags, pennons.

97. The line is quoted, but inaccurately, from Garth's *Dispensary*, Canto 3, where it stands—

 " Where billows never break, nor tempests roar."

98, 99. See note to l. 54 above.

100. **But me**, etc. Cowper had just passed the dreaded month
of January, a month which for him was "accompanied by such
horrors as I have no reason to suppose ever made part of the
experience of any other man. I accordingly look forward to it,
and meet it, with a dread not to be imagined" (*To Newton*,
Feb. 5, 1790).

102. **blasts.** Editions 1798 to 1806 have "winds."

 tempest-tost. Cf. the quotation in note to ll. 88-107 above.

107. **arrive**, a Gallicism for "happen."

108. **My boast**, etc. According to John Johnson's Memoir of
the poet, Mrs. Cowper was "descended by four different lines
from Henry III., King of England."

109. **loins enthroned**, royal progenitors.

112. **Time unrevoked**, without having his "flight reversed";
see l. 74.

117. **Without ... thine**, without being guilty of impairing your
joys; see ll. 84-87.

118, 119. **while the wings ... of thee**, so long as I can call you
up before my imagination and gaze upon this picture of you.

121. **Thyself ... left**, since, though you yourself are gone, your
soothing influence still remains. The line is made up of two
absolute clauses.

EPITAPH ON A HARE.

INTRODUCTION.

This Epitaph was first published in *Poems*, 1800. In a letter
to Bull, March 7, 1783, Cowper writes : " You know.that I kept
two hares. I have written nothing since I saw you but an
epitaph on one of them, which died last week. I send you the
first impression of it." One of the presents sent him by *Anonymous*,
his nameless benefactor, was "a snuff-box of tortoise-shell, with a
beautiful landscape on the lid of it, glazed with crystal, having

the figures of three hares in the foreground, and inscribed above with these words, *The Peasant's Nest*; and below with these, *Tiney, Puss, and Bess*" (*To Lady Hesketh*, Jan. 31, 1786).

The poet gave an account of his hares in the *Gentleman's Magazine* for June, 1784. He says that in 1774, being ill in mind and in body, and wanting some diversion, he had a leveret given him, and afterwards two more. He named them Puss, Tiney, and Bess, and built them a wooden house with three compartments to sleep in. In the daytime they had the range of a hall, and at night each retired to his own bed. Puss soon grew familiar, and became perfectly tame. Not so Tiney, upon whom the kindest treatment had not the least effect. "He too," he writes, "was sick, and in his sickness had an equal share of my attention (with Puss); but if after his recovery I took the liberty to stroke him, he would grunt, strike with his fore feet, spring forward, and bite. He was, however, very entertaining in his way; even his surliness was matter of mirth, and in his play he preserved such an air of gravity, and performed his feats with such solemnity of manner, that in him too I had an agreeable companion." Cowper always admitted them to the parlour after supper, when, the carpet affording their feet a firm hold, they would frisk and bound, and play a thousand gambols.

He says that sow-thistle, dandelion, and lettuce were their favourite vegetables, especially the last. He discovered by accident that they were very fond of fine white sand; he supposed as a digestive. Straw was another of their dainties, and they would feed greedily on oats; but he always made bread their principal nourishment, which was placed every evening in their chambers; for they fed only at evening and in the night. During the winter, when vegetables were not to be got, he mixed this mess of bread with shreds of carrot, adding to it the rind of apples cut extremely thin; for though they were fond of the paring, the apple itself disgusted them. They were also much pleased with twigs of hawthorn.

Bess died young, from having been turned into his box, which had been washed, while it was yet damp; Tiney lived to be nine years old, and died at last, Cowper thought, of some hurt in his loins by a fall. Puss died of mere old age, at the age of eleven years and eleven months. The poet wrote another epitaph in Latin on Tiney.

<h3 style="text-align:center">NOTES.</h3>

1. **whom hound did ne'er pursue.** Cf. *Task*, iii. 334-336 (of Puss):

> "Well—one at least is safe. One sheltered hare
> Has never heard the sanguinary yell
> Of cruel man, exulting in her woes."

Hares are either (1) hunted by men on horseback with a pack of hounds, or (2) coursed with greyhounds—a hare, previously caught, being let loose, and a leash of greyhounds sent after it, to see which greyhound will catch it first.

2. **greyhound** is composed of Icelandic *grey*, a dog, and *hundr*, a hound ; in 'greyhound' therefore 'dog' is repeated twice over. Similar cumulative forms are *touch-wood* (= stick-wood), *jolly-boat* (= yawl-boat), *sledge-hammer* (= hammer-hammer), *reindeer* (= reindeer-deer). Cf. note, p. 71, l. 19.

3. **tainted morning dew**, left its scent on the dewy grass at early morning (when the scent is especially strong).

4. **halloo** (= ah ! lo !) is the huntsman's shout to encourage the hounds. There is also the 'view-halloa,' a cry raised by any one who catches sight of the hare or fox.

7. **to domestic bounds confined.** Cowper used to take Puss out into the garden, but not Tiney.

8. **Jack hare**, probably in the sense of 'saucy hare,' like 'Jacke fool' in Chaucer, rather than in the sense of 'male hare,' like 'jackass.'

10. **pittance**, allowance of food ; generally used of a *small* allowance or portion, a dole. It means lit. *appetising* food, a relish ; whence its derivation.

11. **jealous**, suspicious.

13. **His diet.** See Introduction.

16. **to scour his maw**, to clear out his stomach, by helping his food to digest.

19. **salads failed.** "During the winter, when vegetables were not to be got" (Introduction). *Salad* (Ital. *salato*, p.p. of *salare*, to salt) properly means 'raw herbs cut up and *seasoned*,' but here merely 'green meat.'

29. **five round-rolling moons**, five revolving months. Similarly 'sun' is poetically used for 'year.'

31. **Dozing ... noons**, spending all the middle of the day in sleep.

34, 35. **beguile My heart of**, make my heart forget. In his account of his hares Cowper writes : "In the year 1774, being much indisposed both in mind and body, incapable of diverting myself either with company or books, and yet in a condition that made some diversion necessary, I was glad of anything that would engage my attention without fatiguing it." And he perceived that "in the management of such an animal, I should find just that sort of employment which my case required."

38. **long ... home.** A common phrase for the grave ; cf. Bible, *Eccles.* xii. 5 : "Man goeth to his *long home*, and the mourners go about the streets."

40. gentler. Puss had a much milder disposition than Tiney; see Introduction.

41. shocks, the wear and tear of existence ; the attacks of old age.

44. Must soon, etc. The following memorandum was found among Cowper's papers, dated March 9, 1786 : " This day died poor Puss, aged eleven years eleven months. He died between twelve and one at noon, of mere old age, and apparently without pain." So that Puss survived Tiney almost exactly three years.

THE LOSS OF THE ROYAL GEORGE.

INTRODUCTION.

This dirge was first published in 1803. As is stated in the title, it was written when the news arrived—viz., in September, 1782—to the music of the March in *Scipio*, an opera by Handel, this March being an air which Lady Austen was accustomed to play on the harpsichord. In a letter to Unwin, August 4, 1783, to whom he had sent the poem with a Latin version, Cowper writes : " I am glad you were pleased with my Latin ode, and indeed with my English dirge, as much as I was myself. The tune laid me under a disadvantage, obliging me to write in Alexandrines ; which I suppose would suit no ear but a French one ; neither did I intend anything more than that the subject and the words should be sufficiently accommodated to the music." But, as Canon Benham remarks, " by common consent he has produced one of the noblest songs in the language." " Alexandrines " are hexameter lines of twelve, thirteen, or fourteen syllables, often divided by a pause into two parts between the sixth and the seventh syllable. Thus the last stanza of the dirge, written as a couplet, runs thus :

" But Kem|penfelt | is gone, ‖ his vic|tories | are o'er ;
   And he | and his | eight hundred ‖ shall plough | the wave | no
      more."

On the morning of August 29, 1782, the " Royal George," of 108 guns, while being careened at Spithead, Portsmouth harbour, heeled over in a sudden gust of wind, and sank instantly. She had nearly 1100 souls on board, including many women and children and others who were taking leave of their friends. Of these some 800 were lost. Rear-Admiral Richard Kempenfeldt went down with his flag-ship. He was about to sail to join the fleet for the relief of Gibraltar.

NOTES.

1. **Toll.** Church bells are tolled on the occasion of the death of persons of importance. Cf. Tennyson's *Ode on the Death of the Duke of Wellington*, 53, 58 : " Let the bell be toll'd."

4. **Fast by,** close to. Cf. note, p. 83, l. 47.

5. **Eight hundred,** the crew of the vessel.

7. **heel.** The ship was careened or laid on her side to repair a pipe situated below the water line.

9. **A land-breeze.** The gust came from the land side, and so overturned the vessel in deep water. The " shrouds " are the ropes and tackling that support the masts.

12. **all her crew.** About 300, however, of the ship's company were saved.

14. **Kempenfelt.** See Introduction.

21, 22. **His sword ... pen.** He was sitting in his cabin at the time, engaged in writing.

25. **Weigh the vessel up.** In a letter to Hill, October 20, 1783, Cowper writes : " I must beg leave ... to mourn equally that the Royal George cannot be weighed : the rather, because I wrote two poems, one Latin and one English, to encourage the attempt." Attempts were made in 1782 and 1783 to " weigh " or raise the ship by passing huge cables under the keel, but were unsuccessful. In 1839-42 the wreck was blown up piece-meal by charges of gunpowder fired by electricity, under the superintendence of Sir Charles Pasley.

26. **Once dreaded by our foes.** The " Royal George " had previously been the flag-ship of Admirals Anson, Boscawen, Rodney, and Hawke, all celebrated for their naval victories over the French.

27. **mingle with our cup,** *i.e.* eating and drinking—the common concerns of life—ought to be accompanied by a sense of sorrow at our loss.

31. **Full charged ... thunder,** with her complete equipment of cannon. Cf. *Boadicea*, 27, and note to *Ibid.* 25.

ON THE SHORTNESS OF HUMAN LIFE.

INTRODUCTION.

Cowper enclosed this translation (first published in 1803) to Newton on January 25, 1784. He prefaced it with a copy of

the Latin original by Dr. Jortin, and the following playful
introduction :

> " The late Doctor Jortin
> Had the good fortune
> To write these verses
> Upon tombs and hearses,
> Which I, being jinglish,
> Have done into English."

The original had been sent by Unwin to Cowper, who writes to
him, January, 1784 : " It occurred to me that perhaps you would
not be displeased with an attempt to give a poetical translation
of the lines you sent me.   They are so beautiful that I felt the
temptation irresistible. ... It is a beautiful composition.   It is
tender, touching, and elegant.   It is not easy to do it justice in
English."

Dr. John Jortin, an eminent scholar and divine, was born in
1698, educated at Cambridge, and became prebendary of St.
Paul's and Archdeacon of London.   He is the author of several
theological and other works.   He died in 1770.

NOTES.

3. **that orient day subdues**, whose light is dimmed by the bright-
ness of day.   *Orient* (Lat. *orient-*, stem of *oriens*, ' the rising sun,
the east '), ' eastern,' means ' bright ' here rather than ' dawn-
ing '; it represents the *purpurei*, ' brilliant,' of the original Latin.
Milton frequently uses *orient* for ' bright '; cf. *Par. Lost*, i. 545,
546 :

> " Ten thousand banners rise into the air
> With *orient* colours waving."

6. **genial** has here its earlier meaning of ' productive ' (Lat.
gi-g(e)nere, ' to beget ') ;. cf. Milton, *Par. Lost*, vii. 279-282) :

> " Main Ocean flow'd, not idle, but with warm
> Prolific humour softening all her globe,
> Fermented the great Mother to conceive,
> Satiate with *genial* moisture."

9. **Zephyr**, the warm west wind.

16. **Still 'tis winter**, etc.   Man dies and is buried, and there is
no more revival for him.   *Still* means ' always.'

THE VALEDICTION.

INTRODUCTION.

The latter half of this poem (l. 49 to end) was published by
Hayley in 1803, Thurlow being then alive (Colman had died in

1794). After Thurlow's death in 1806 there was no longer any reason for suppressing the former half, and the complete poem was published by Southey in 1835.

When Cowper published his first volume [1] on March 1, 1782, he sent copies to a few of his friends, among whom were Thurlow, then Lord Chancellor (to whom he also addressed a letter), and Colman, proprietor and manager of the Haymarket Theatre. Neither took any notice of the gift, and on March 18 he expresses to Unwin his doubt of receiving an answer from " his Chancellorship," who, he continues, " is so busy a man ... that I am forced to mortify myself with the thought that both my book and my letter may be thrown into a corner as too insignificant for a statesman's notice." On April 1 he writes to Unwin that when Hill had an opportunity of conversing with Thurlow in private, " my poor authorship was not so much as mentioned : whence I learn two lessons ; first, that however important I may be in my own eyes, I am very insignificant in his ; and secondly, that I am never likely to receive any acknowledgment of the favours I have conferred upon his Lordship, either under his own hand or by means of a third person ; and consequently that our intercourse has ceased for ever." Accordingly, in a letter to Unwin, November 10, 1783, he enclosed *The Valediction*, with the injunction that the verses were not for the press, and remarking that " the unkind behaviour of our acquaintance will sometimes obtrude itself upon us with an importunity not easily to be resisted "; and he goes on: " In such a moment it was that I conceived this poem, and gave loose to a degree of resentment which perhaps I ought not to have indulged, but which in a cooler hour I cannot altogether condemn. My former intimacy with the two characters (see General Introduction) was such, that I could not but feel myself provoked by the neglect with which they both treated me on a late occasion." In a subsequent letter to Unwin, November 24, 1783, he writes in reference to these verses : " A man's lordship is nothing to me. ... If he thinks himself privileged by it to treat me with neglect, I am his humble servant, and shall never be at a loss to render him an equivalent. I am, however, most angry with the manager. He has published a book [2] since he received mine, and has not vouchsafed to send it me ; a requital which good manners, not to say the remembrance of former friendship, ought to have suggested."

The stern dignity and trenchant force of this poem remind us of Samuel Johnson's famous letter to the Earl of Chesterfield shortly after the publication of his Dictionary (see Boswell's *Life of Johnson*, I. 261).

---

[1] It is deserving of note that Cowper's stanzas *On the Promotion of Thurlow to the Chancellorship* were included in this volume ; see his letter to Thurlow in note to l. 20 below.

[2] A translation of Horace's *Ars Poetica.*

2. **exhale,** reduce to vapour, dry up. The verb has a causative meaning here.

4. **Cold in his cause,** indifferent to his interests.

5. **adieu.** See note, p. 110, l. 31, *ad fin.*

6. **Cold in my turn,** etc. Cf. *To Unwin,* Nov. 24, 1783: "They think of me as of the man in the moon.... Upon that point we are agreed, our indifference is mutual, and were I to publish again, which is not impossible, I should give them a proof of it." Cowper accordingly sent his second volume to neither; but he was not the man to cherish resentment, and when he was engaged upon the publication of his Homer, he wrote to both. From Colman he received "the most affectionate letter imaginable"; and a "very kind" letter from Thurlow was forwarded to him through Lady Hesketh, which opened the way for a renewal of their intercourse.

7. **Niger,** Latin for "black," represents Thurlow, in reference to his dark, almost swarthy, complexion.

9. **brain well furnished.** Cf. *Task,* iv. 209: "the void of an *unfurnished* (*i.e.* empty) brain"; and *The Progress of Error,* 425: "Hence an *unfurnished* and a listless mind." And *To Unwin,* July 27, 1780: "First came the barber; who, after having embellished the outside of my head, has left the inside just as *unfurnished* as he found it. Also Tennyson, *Freedom,* x.:

" Men loud against all forms of power—
Unfurnished brows, tempestuous tongues."

tongue well taught. Thurlow was a ready and powerful speaker, and as a conversationalist, was a match for Dr. Johnson himself, who confessed that he would "prepare himself for no man in England but Lord Thurlow."

10. **press,** maintain, emphasise.

11. **senatorial,** statesmanlike. Thurlow's features were severe and impressive. Fox once made the remark that "no man could be so wise as Thurlow looked."

12. **Sound sense.** Gibbon, describing the appearance of the Treasury-bench in 1774, speaks of "the majestic sense of Thurlow."

intrepid spirit. At school Thurlow had the reputation of being "a daring, refractory, clever boy," and at college he was at war with all the authorities. He carried the same combative disposition into political life, where he was remarkable for his frankness and unflinching courage.

14. **Made you a peer.** Thurlow became Lord Chancellor on June 3, 1778, when he was raised to the peerage as Baron Thurlow

of Ashfield in Suffolk, the parish where his father had been vicar.

15. **Pretend to**, claims. So in 'The Young Pretender,' *pretender* = claimant.

parts, abilities.

19. **verse**. His first volume of poetry ; see Introduction.

20. **a modest sheet.** The letter that accompanied the volume. It ran thus :—

"Olney, Bucks, Feb. 25, 1782.

My Lord,—I make no apology for what I account a duty: I should offend against the cordiality of our former friendship should I send a volume into the world, and forget how much I am bound to pay my particular respects to your lordship upon that occasion. When we parted you little thought of hearing from me again; and I as little that I should live to write to you, still less that I should wait on you in the capacity of an author.

Among the pieces I have the honour to send, there is one for which I must entreat your pardon. I mean that of which your Lordship is the subject. The best excuse I can make is, that it flowed almost spontaneously from the affectionate remembrance of a connexion that did me so much honour.

As to the rest, their merits, if they have any, and their defects, which are probably more than I am aware of, will neither of them escape your notice. But where there is much discernment, there is generally much candour ; and I commit myself into your Lordship's hands, with the less anxiety, being well acquainted with yours.

If my first visit, after so long an interval should prove neither a troublesome nor a dull one, but especially if not altogether an unprofitable one, *omne tuli punctum.*

I have the honour to be, though with very different impressions of some subjects, yet with the same sentiments of affection and esteem as ever, your Lordship's faithful and most obedient, humble servant,

W. C."

21. **to recall a promise.** In 1762, when he was studying at the Temple, Cowper said one evening to Thurlow, " Thurlow, I am nobody, and shall be always nobody, and you will be chancellor. You shall provide for me when you are." Upon which Thurlow smiled and replied, " I surely will."

23. **to comply with feelings**, to gratify my own kind feelings towards you.

27. **a meaner stage.** Colman's occupation, as manager of a theatre, is put on a lower level than Thurlow's.

28. **Amusement-monger**, dealer in amusement. *Monger* is from O. E. *mangian*, 'to traffic,' lit. 'to deal in a *mixture* of things,' connected with *mengan*, 'to mingle.'

29. **histrionic patentee**, holder of a patent or license as manager of a theatre. Theatres were licensed by Act of Parliament in 1737. " Illustrious " is said ironically.

30. **Terentius.** Cowper's name for Colman, as being a playwriter, and perhaps also as having translated the comedies of Terentius, a celebrated Roman comic poet, who lived about B.C. 195-158.

33. born a gentleman. Colman's father was British envoy at Florence, and his mother was sister to the Countess of Bath. Educated at Westminster School and at Christchurch, Oxford, he was intended for the legal profession.

34. buskin, sock, and raree-show. The *buskin* (Lat. *cothurnus*) was a high-heeled boot worn by Greek tragic actors, to add to their height and dignity ; the *sock* (Lat. *soccus*) was a kind of thin-soled slipper worn by comic actors. Hence the words "buskin" and "sock" were used to denote Tragedy and Comedy respectively ; as here " by buskin, sock " means 'by the representation of tragedies and comedies.' So Milton (*Il Penseroso*, 102) uses "the buskined stage" for 'the tragic drama,' and speaks (*L'Allegro*, 132) of "Jonson's learned sock" in allusion to his comedies. For *raree-show*, see note, p. 75, l. 16 ; it means here a stage-pageant of any kind.

35. school-fellow and partner. In apposition to "I" in l. 39.

plays, school-games.

36. Nichol. Dr. Nichol was head-master of Westminster School when Cowper and Colman were there.

swung ... bays, dealt out punishments for wrong-doing and rewards for good scholarship. Among the ancients, success in poetry was rewarded by a laurel crown ("the bays"), and it was the old custom in our universities for graduates in rhetoric and poetry to be presented with a laurel wreath.

38. The weekly censor, etc. An allusion to *The Connoisseur*, a weekly periodical which was started by Colman and Bonnell Thornton in January, 1754, and to which Cowper contributed five papers. It came to a close in 1756. It was modelled upon *The Spectator*, its aim being a good-humoured attack upon the follies and failings of society at the time.

40. Graced with the name, *i.e.* with Cowper's name on the title-page.

41. prove, 'turn out to be,' as again in l. 71, below.   Cf. note, p. 131, l. 56.

44. a dream.   Cf. note, p. 94, l. 19.

45, 46. strutting ... Who fret their hour. A reminiscence of Shaks. *Macbeth*, v. v. 24, 25 :

     " Life's but a walking shadow, a poor player
       That struts and frets his hour upon the stage."

Fret their hour means 'are full of passion and excitement for the brief time that they are acting their parts.' *Hour* is to be parsed as an adverbial objective.

45. school of queens and kings. Colman, as theatrical manager, would superintend the performances of plays in many of which the parts of kings or queens would occur.

47. **cold distemper of the day**, the heartless indifference which is a characteristic of the present age.

51. **our unsuspecting years**, our youth, when we have no suspicion that our friends may fail us.

52. **The promise**, etc. We then look forward to the increase and development of our friendships.

57. **the expected harvest lost**, *i.e.* the loss of the expected harvest.

58. **Decayed ... frost.** Either the lapse of time gradually puts an end to the friendship, or some sudden rupture occurs. For the metaphor contained in ll. 51-58, cf. Shaks. *Henry VIII.* III. ii. 352-358 :

> " This is the state of man : to-day he puts forth
> The tender leaves of hopes ; to-morrow blossoms,
> And bears his blushing honours thick upon him ;
> The third day comes a frost, a killing frost,
> And, when he thinks, good easy man, full surely
> His greatness is a-ripening, nips his root,
> And then he falls, as I do."

60. **renewed in nature.** Cf. l. 67. The heart of man is by nature unequal to the demands of true friendship, and requires to be changed and renovated by divine grace. To be a true friend, a man must first be a true Christian.

66. **And wet his cheeks**, etc. Cf. the Biblical precept of sympathy, *Rom.* xii. 15 : " Weep with them that weep."

70. **Starts ... bow.** Man's heart fails to respond to the strain put upon it, like a bow that snaps when you pull the string.

74. **bustle life away**, spend their lives in the restless pursuit of business or pleasure.

76. **thunder-clouds**, gloomy threatenings of ill ; anxieties.

77. **the charge of**, under the care of ; *i.e.* let me be so blest as to find. The notion that human beings are attended by their ' guardian angels ' is a common one and based on Bible, *Matthew*, xviii. 10.

78. **One who has known**, etc., *i.e.* one who has mixed in society without being affected by its follies and weaknesses ; cf. the two following lines.

81. **With him, perhaps with her.** There can, I think, be little doubt that Lady Austen (rather than Mrs. Unwin, who does not fit into the description given in ll. 78-80) is here alluded to as fulfilling Cowper's ideal of a friend. He had made her acquaintance in the summer of 1781, and though in February, 1782, a fracas had taken place between them, the breach was soon healed, and the two were as friendly as ever at the time

when *The Valediction* was written.   The final rupture came in the spring of 1784.

82. **the fair.** See note, p. 70, l. 26.

83. **unthought-of,** unknown to the world, sequestered.

84. **All former friends** (being) **forgiven,** etc.   An absolute clause.

86. **Union of hearts.** Possibly Cowper had Newton's lines, referring to Cowper himself, in his mind :

> "I had a friend beloved, and well he knew
>   *Union of heart*, confiding, fond, and true."

92. **crowns,** renders complete.

93. **giving one,** etc. If He gives not only a friend, but a friend whose affection is set on heavenly things.

94. **Born from above,** with his nature renewed and sanctified by Divine grace ; cf. l. 60.   This change of heart is represented as a "new birth" in Bible, *John,* iii. 5, where Christ says : "Except a man be *born anew* (Revised Version), he cannot see the kingdom of God," where the marginal reading for "born anew" is "born from above."

95. **bankrupt Nature,** *i.e.* Nature unable to supply a true friend.

96. **Whose noblest coin,** etc., the best that she can give is man as he is by nature, frail and unreliable.   The genuine, sterling friend is God's gift.

97. **Ophir** was the place whence Hiram, king of Tyre, brought much gold to Solomon ; see Bible, 1 *Kings,* ix. 28, etc.

98. **A soul,** etc., a soul that has been stamped with the Divine image, *i.e.* made like God. Cf. Bible, *Col.* iii. 10 : "(Ye) have put on the new man, which is renewed in knowledge after the image of him that created him " ; also 2 *Cor.* iii. 18.

GRATITUDE.

INTRODUCTION.

These verses were first published in 1803.   The original poem, as sent to Lady Hesketh, bore the title "Benefactions.   A Poem in Shenstone's manner.   Addressed to my dear coz, April 14, 1788."   In this copy Cowper subsequently made considerable alterations, omitting one stanza, the sixth, and substituting two other stanzas for the last two of the original, in which the last stanza but one runs thus :

" These items endear my abode,
  Disposing me oft to reflect
By whom they were kindly bestowed,
  Whom here I impatient expect.
But hush! She a parent attends,
  Whose dial-hand points to eleven,
Who, oldest and dearest of friends,
  Waits only a passage to Heaven."

Now, at this time Cowper was expecting a visit from Lady Hesketh, which was delayed by the illness of her father, who died in the following June ; so that both the original title of the poem and internal evidence show that, as it originally stood, it was written in 1788.[1] The revised version of it was written some time before March 12, 1790, since in a letter of that date to Mrs. King, Cowper says : " This reminds me of a piece in your possession, which I will entreat you to commit to the flames, because I am somewhat ashamed of it. To make you amends, I hereby promise to send you a new edition of it when time shall serve, delivered from the passages that I dislike in the first, and in other respects amended. The piece that I mean is one entitled, ' To Lady Hesketh on her furnishing for me our house at Weston '—or, as the lawyers say, words to that amount."

When Lady Hesketh visited the poet in the summer of 1786, she arranged for his and Mrs. Unwin's removal from Orchard Side, their house at Olney, to Weston Lodge in the neighbouring village of Weston Underwood, she herself undertaking the expenses of removal and providing new furniture for the larger house ; and it is in reference to this friendly liberality on her part that this poem was composed.

NOTES.

1. **This cap.** The poet's calico or cambric muslin caps, which he wore when writing, have become famous from Romney's and Lawrence's well-known portraits, in both of which he is represented in one of them. One of these caps is still in the possession of Canon W. Cowper Johnson, Rector of Northwold, Norfolk.

5. **my cousin.** The first copy has " my Harriet," that being Lady Hesketh's Christian name.

7. **Wreathed,** twisted.

9. **wheel-footed,** *i.e.* it ran on casters.

---

[1] All previous editions, as far as I am aware, give 1786 as the date when this poem was written.

12. **scribble and doze** answer to "toil and repose" in l. 10 above.

13. **Bright-studded,** edged with ornamental brass-headed nails. The first copy has :

> "Thick-studded with bordering nails
> Smooth-headed and gilded and bright
> As Vesper, who when the day fails,
> Adorns the dark forehead of Night."

14. **rival** is a noun here. His study chair with its row of bright nails was a rival of the constellation Cassiopeia or Cassiope, popularly known as "The Lady in the Chair," because the chief stars of the constellation form the outline of a chair. Milton (*Il Penseroso*, 19) alludes to Cassiope as "that starr'd Ethiop queen."

15. **or** is equivalent to 'otherwise' here.

18. **Caledonia's traffic,** manufactured at Paisley, near Glasgow. Caledonia is the ancient name for Scotland.

19. **knights of the boot,** fox-hunters or horsemen generally. Cowper calls them "knights of the boot" from their distinguishing characteristic ; just as Don Quixote called himself 'The Knight of the Sorrowful Countenance.' In Cowper's time a "boot" meant a riding-boot which came up to the knee.

20. **Escaped from,** etc., just come from a ride across country. The first copy has :

> "Dirt-splash'd in a cross-country ride."

21. **mirror within.** The table seems to have been made with a flap, which lifted and disclosed a looking-glass on its underside, which was thus safe from being broken or soiled ("secure from collision and dust").

24. **periwig.** See note, p. 104, l. 75.

nicely, accurately ; cf. *The Needless Alarm*, 63, and note.

25. **movable,** *i.e.* the bookcase was not a fixture in the wall.

27. **charged,** filled, loaded ; as in 'to *charge* a gun.'

octavos and twelves, volumes of octavo and duodecimo sizes. In the former, the sheet is folded into *eight*, in the latter, into *twelve* leaves.

29. **flaming,** etc., *i.e.* bound in red leather stamped in gold.

30. **My poems.** His two volumes ; the first, comprising the *Moral Satires*, etc., published in 1782, and the second, the *Task*, etc., published in 1785. His translation of Homer appeared in July, 1791 ; it was begun in November, 1784, and completed in August, 1790, so that he was engaged upon it at this time.

33. **the alcove.** An *alcove* (of Arabic derivation) is a recess in a room, often occupied by a cupboard or side-board ("buffet").

34. Which here ... buffet. In the first copy :

"Which mortals have named a beaufette."

Notice that Cowper anglicises the pronunciation of *buffet*, making its last syllable rhyme with *yet*.

35, 36. what the gods ... yet. Cowper jokes upon the fine name *buffet* for a sideboard, intimating that the celestials may have some finer name still for it.

38. as the season demands. They keep out the sun in summer and the cold in winter.

40. Mulciber's hands. *Mulciber* is a surname of Vulcan, the fire-god and worker in metals ; from Lat. *mulcere*, to soften or melt (iron, etc.).

46. our perishing kind, mortal men ; mankind subject to decay.

50. chattels. *Chattel* is a doublet of *cattle*, and both are from the Low Lat. *capitale, captale*, capital, property.

of leisure, that belong to or promote leisure.

52. such fancies, such light pieces as the present poem.

53. fancies I fear, etc., 'I fear my description of my study furniture will indeed seem imaginary and not real, since poets seldom own such fine things.' Poets are or were regarded as proverbially poor ; cf. *To Lady Hesketh*, July 28, 1788 : "I join with you, my dearest coz, in wishing that I owned the fee simple of all the beautiful scenes around you, but such emoluments were never designed for poets."

THE MORNING DREAM.

INTRODUCTION.

This poem was written in 1788, and published in *Poems*, 1803. In a letter to General Cowper, March, 1788, enclosing these verses, the poet writes : "When the condition of our negroes in the islands was first presented to me as a subject for songs, I felt myself not at all allured to the undertaking ; it seemed to offer only images of horror, which could by no means be accommodated to the style of that sort of composition." He goes on to say that having a desire to comply with the request made him, he at last produced three, and "that which appears to myself the best of those three, I have sent you." In a letter to Lady Hesketh, March 31, 1788, he says : "I have written one more song, and sent it. It is called the Morning Dream, and may be sung to the tune of Tweed-Side, or any other tune that will suit it." The three mentioned above are *The Negro's*

Complaint, Sweet Meat has Sour Sauce, and *The Morning Dream* ; a fourth, *Pity for Poor Africans,* was written subsequently. On April, 1792, Cowper's lines *To William Wilberforce* were published in the *Northampton Mercury,* "attested," he writes to Lady Hesketh, April 26, 1792, "with my name at length, in order to clear my character from a calumny that had spread all over the country concerning my real opinion of the slave trade."

In his poem of *Charity* (ll. 137-179), written in 1781, Cowper had denounced the slave trade, and in May, 1787, the Society for its Suppression was founded, of which Thomas Clarkson and William Wilberforce were prominent members. In May, 1788, Wilberforce made the first motion in the House of Commons on the subject. In 1807, an Act was passed for the Abolition of the Slave Trade. In 1834, an Act was passed for the Abolition of Slavery itself in all British Colonies, and 770,280 slaves were set free, a sum of £20,000,000 being voted as compensation to the slave-owners.

NOTES.

1. **spring.** The poet chooses the spring-time for his happy dream, as being the season of hope and promise.

2. **Asleep** = 'on sleep,' as in *abed, aboard, ashore, afloat* (l. 5).

   at the dawn. Perhaps an allusion to the belief that dreams dreamt just before dawn are true.

3. **I cannot but sing,** I cannot do anything except sing; I must sing or turn into verse. Cf. l. 41.

6. **hence to the westward,** from England towards the West Indies. It was mainly in our West Indian Colonies that slavery was practised, shiploads of negroes being imported thither from Africa (see l. 32) to work on the sugar and cotton plantations, since native labour was inadequate, and European labour was impossible in that tropical climate. Jamaica was almost ruined by the emancipation of the slaves.

9. **steerage,** the part of the ship where the steering is done, the stern.

   a woman. Britannia, who is imaged as an armed lady, sitting with a shield by her side (see the reverse of a penny). Cf. l. 45.

12. **taught me,** such as no woman ever made me feel before.

17. **to a strain,** so as effectively to produce it ; singing it loud and clear.

20. **her glory,** her glorious or radiant form.

23. **methought.** See note, p. 74, l. 13. For **sung,** see note, p. 83, l. 60.

24. **'Twas liberty**, etc., merely to listen to her song was as delightful as liberty itself.

25. **dividing**, cleaving the water with ship's keel. So we speak of *ploughing* the waves for sailing over them.

26. **slave-cultured**, cultivated by slaves. *Cultured* usually means cultivated in a moral sense, as in 'a cultured mind.'

island. One of the West Indies, as Jamaica.

28. **Oppression** (being) **his terrible name.** An absolute clause.

30. **hung with lashes.** A sort of cat-o'-nine-tails, which consisted of nine lengths of cord fastened to a thick rope.

31. **his prey,** *i.e.* the negroes. In 1807 it was shown that since 1792 more than 3½ millions of Africans had been torn from their country, and had either perished on the "middle passage" (the voyage from Africa to the West Indies) or been sold in the West Indies.

33. **soon as**, short for 'as soon as.'

approaching agrees with "woman" in the next line.

36. **his subjects,** *i.e.* the slaves.

38. **the moment,** *i.e.* at the moment at which. *Moment* is to be parsed as an adverbial objective.

40. **with rapture inspired**, filled with an ecstasy of joy.

41. **how could I but muse**, how could I help musing ; see note to l. 3 above.

42. **betide** seems to mean 'forebode' here. It properly means to befall, to happen.

44. **Which served ... guide**, which helped my puzzled mind to explain the dream.

45. **o'er the waves**, wherever her ships sail. A slave when once on board of a British ship was free. The legal decision that slavery could not exist in Great Britain was given in June, 1772.

47. **black-sceptred** implies a harsh, gloomy, and wicked sway, as we might call a reign of love 'golden-sceptred.'

rulers of slaves, those who allow slavery in their dominions.

48. **Resolves** etc. But this prophecy was not fulfilled till August 28, 1833, when an act was passed for the abolition of slavery throughout the British Colonies, the abolition coming into force on August 1, 1834, while the day of the actual emancipation of the slaves was August 1, 1838.

THE RETIRED CAT.

INTRODUCTION.

This poem appears to have been written in 1791, and was first published in 1803. Cats were included among Cowper's pets, and when he was removed to the St. Albans Asylum his favourite cat was entrusted to Hill, to whom he writes after his recovery (November 8, 1765): "Stroke puss's back the wrong way and it will put her in mind of her master." In a letter to Lady Hesketh, November 10, 1787, he says: "I have a kitten, my dear, the drollest of all creatures that ever wore a cat's skin. Her gambols are not to be described, and would be incredible if they could. In point of size she is likely to be a kitten always, being extremely small of her age, but time, I suppose, that spoils everything, will make her also a cat. You will see her, I hope, before that melancholy period shall arrive, for no wisdom that she may gain by experience and reflection hereafter, will compensate the loss of her present hilarity. She is dressed in a tortoise-shell suit, and I know that you will delight in her."

NOTES.

3. **addicted to inquire**, a poetical license. Strictly we should say ' addicted to inquiring.'

8, 9. **Nature ... philosophique**, perhaps she had this contemplative disposition implanted in her by Nature. For the figure, cf. Tennyson, *To J. S.*, 3, 4:

> "Gently comes the world to those
> That are cast in gentle *mould*."

Philosophique=philosophic or philosophical. Cf. note, p. 75, l. 23. Our older writers often employ the French termination in -*que* in place of the English in -*c*. Thus Bacon (*Essay on Love*) writes " reciproque " for "reciprocal"; and Macaulay has " relique " (for "relic"), a form which Wordsworth seems always to have used. We still write both *lacquey* and *lackey*.

11. **debonair** = Fr. *de bon aire*, of a good mien or appearance; elegant, mannerly.

13. **with convenience**, conveniently, comfortably.

17, 18. **wanting ... To seem**, *i.e.* if she had only had a fan, she would have seemed, etc. *Save*, now parsed as a preposition, is really an adjective (from Fr. *sauf*, Lat. *salvus*) used absolutely; thus "save my fan" = 'my fan being safe or reserved.' Both Shakspere and Milton write "save *he*," retaining the absolute use.

18. **nymph.**   See notes, p. 96, l. 1 ; p. 106, l. 7.   The *sedan* or *sedan-chair*, a portable vehicle carried by two men, was named from *Sedan*, a town in France.   It was first seen in England in 1581, and came into very general use in 1649.   It was a common conveyance in Cowper's day.   Cf. *Task*, i. 755 ; *Tirocinium*, 748.

20. **to court,** to a royal reception or ' drawing-room.'

27. **utensil.**   Observe the accentuation—*utensil* instead of the ordinary *utensil*.   Cf. Milton, *Paradise Regained*, iii. 336 :

> " And waggons fraught with *utensils* of war."

And Wordsworth, *Michael*, 115 :

> " An aged *utensil*, which had performed."

Cowper also throws the accent back in *empirics* (*Task*. ii. 352) for "empirics," and in *cément* (*Ib*. v. 147) for "cemént." Cf. note, p. 92, l. 142.

32. **wanton,** play, sport.   See note, p. 106, l. 9.

37. **such as merchants,** etc., *i.e.* India muslin.   The invention of the ' mule ' spinning machine in 1779 gave birth to the manufacture of British muslin.

40. **chest,** the aperture into which the drawer is inserted.

46. **humdrum song,** the cat's purr.   *Humdrum*, a compound of *hum* and *drum*, means ' droning, monotonous.'

48. **as she would sleep her last,** as though she would never wake again.   In "sleep her last (sleep)" there is an ellipse of the cognate object, as in ' He did his best (doing),' ' He tried his hardest (trying).'

49. **housewifely inclined,** intent on household duties.

54. **attended,** waited upon.   Cf. l. 66 below.

56. **to prove** is often used in eighteenth century poetry for ' to be,' as in Gay's Fable where the lover says, " How happy should I *prove*, Might I " etc.   Cf. *The Valediction*, 41, 71.

59. **'kerchiefs,** short for ' handkerchiefs '; but the apostrophe is unnecessary.   *Kerchief* = O. Fr. *couvre-chef*, *i.e.* ' cover-head ' or head-cover, being originally used to cover the head.   Cf. *curfew*.

62. **Sol,** Latin for ' sun,' for which it is used in mock-heroic fashion.

69, 70. **sprightly ... gray.**   Conventional epithets, keeping up the mock-heroic style of the piece.

74. **presaged approaching doom,** thought she should soon die.

75. **slept a ... wink.**   See note, p. 75, l. 14.

76. **jeopardy** is O. Fr. *jeu parti*, ' a divided game,' *i.e.* a game in which the chances are even, a game of hazard ; hence ' hazard, danger.'

77. **watching**, being awake. Cf. Milton, *Paradise Lost*, vii. 106 : "Sleep listening to thee will *watch*," *i.e.* keep awake; and Shaks. *Hamlet*, II. ii. 147, 148 : "(He) fell into a sadness, then into a fast, Thence to a *watch*," *i.e.* sleeplessness; and *Ib.* III. ii. 263 : "Some must *watch*, while some must sleep."

79. **went pit-a-pat**, palpitated (with alarm).

84. **chest**, here the chest of drawers.

92. **'gan.** See note, p. 103, l. 44.

100. **erst**, at first, before. *Er-st* is the superlative of *ere*, M.E. *er*, soon, before. Cf. *early*, soon-like.

   airy, buoyant, jaunty.

101. **fond apprehension**, foolish opinion.

104. **hyperbolical**, extravagant, high-flown.

115. **in school of tribulation**, taught by suffering. *Tribulation* is from Lat. *tribulum*, a corn-thresher, whence we have *tribulare*, *tribulatum*, to thresh out corn, and so to oppress, afflict.

EPITAPH ON "FOP."

INTRODUCTION.

This piece was written at Eartham, in August, 1792, and first published in 1803. In a letter, enclosing it, to Mrs. Courtenay, August 25, 1792, Cowper writes : "I send my dear Catherina the epitaph she desired, composed as well as I could compose it in a place where every object, being still new to me, distracts my attention, and makes me as awkward at verse as if I had never dealt in it." In a subsequent letter to the same, Sept. 10, 1792, he says : "I am proud that you are pleased with the Epitaph I sent you, and shall be prouder to see it perpetuated by the chisel. It is all that I have done since here I came, and all that I have been able to do ... I find, like the man in the fable, who could leap only at Rhodes, that verse is almost impossible to me except at Weston." This epitaph was "perpetuated by the chisel" by being inscribed on the pedestal of the monumental urn to "Fop," erected in the "Wilderness" in the grounds of the Throck-mortons at Weston Underwood, where it may still be read.

Mrs. Catherine (Cowper's "Catherina") Courtenay was the wife of Mr. George Courtenay, to whom she (then Miss Stapleton) was married in June, 1792. He was the younger brother of John Throckmorton ; but, upon John's succeeding to the title in 1791 by the death of Sir Robert Throckmorton of Bucklands, Berk-shire, adopted his second name of Courtenay as a surname, and in March, 1792, came to reside at Weston Hall. She was most helpful to Cowper in making a fair copy of his Homer. Upon the death of Sir John Throckmorton, without issue, in 1819, George succeeded to the title, and Mrs. Courtenay became Lady Throckmorton.

NOTES.

1. **though Fop by name,** *i.e.* the name "Fop" might imply that he was merely a handsome dog, a dandy, undeserving of honour.

2. **Moulders,** decays, turns to dust. *Mould* is crumbling soil from a root *mal*, to bruise.

3. **No sycophant,** etc., *i.e.* not a servile flatterer, though he is a spaniel, a kind of dog that is noted for its fawning behaviour. *Sycophant* is the Gk. συκοφάντης, lit. a ' fig-shewer,' perhaps one who informs against exporters of figs ; hence, a common informer, a sneak. For *spaniel*, see note, p. 106, l. 5, *ad fin.*

4. **a martyr to the chase.** See l. 8 below. The *hound* was the dog used in hunting ; cf. *The Needless Alarm*, 33. Fop was fond of chasing rabbits, etc., on his own account.

9. **shade,** ghost. Pope frequently uses *shade* for the soul separated from the body.

TO MRS. UNWIN.

INTRODUCTION.

This sonnet was first published in 1803. Southey, and subsequent editors of Cowper, give May, 1793, as the date of its composition, but the letter to Mrs. King, March 12, 1790 (see Introduction to *On the Receipt of my Mother's Picture*, p. 108), appears to prove that it must have been written at some time previous to the date of that letter. The only alternative, viz., that the poet there refers to some other poem addressed to Mrs. Unwin (for internal evidence alone excludes the verses *To Mary*) which has not come down to us, is very improbable. The tone of this poem is, besides, more appropriate to the period before Mrs. Unwin's paralytic seizure in 1791 ; see Introduction to *To Mary*, p. 134.

In connexion with it may be quoted the beautiful reference to Mrs. Unwin in the *Task*, i. 144-149 :

" And witness, dear companion of my walks,
   Whose arm this twentieth winter I perceive
   Fast locked in mine, with pleasure such as Love,

Confirmed by long experience of thy worth
And well-tried virtues, could alone inspire—
Witness a joy that thou hast doubled long."

Compare also *The Winter Nosegay*, included in Cowper's first volume.

NOTES.

1. **a lyre with other strings,** *i.e.* a higher poetical faculty than I now possess.

2. **feigned they drew.** Thus Orpheus (see note, p. 98, l. 62) claimed to be the son of Apollo. Cf. Pope, *Messiah*, 5, 6:

"O Thou my voice inspire
Who touched Isaiah's hallowed lips with fire."

3. **new,** fresh and untainted.

4. **by praise of,** *i.e.* by having praised.

5. **I shed my wings,** I lose my poetical powers. We speak of 'poetical *flights*,' and similarly Milton's "adventurous song," in *Par. Lost*. i. 14, "With no middle flight intends to soar."

8. **immortalizes.** Cf. *The Castaway*, 53, 54, and note.

9. **a book.** Reference to God's "book" or register of the good, sometimes called the "book of life," is frequent in the Bible. We have also God's "books," containing men's good and bad actions: see *Rev.* xx. 12.

TO MARY.

INTRODUCTION.

The "Mary" of this poem, written in the autumn of 1793, shortly before Cowper finally left Weston, and first published in 1803, is Mrs. Unwin, the almost life-long companion of the poet. See General Introduction, p. x. In December, 1791, she was seized with paralysis, from which she recovered slowly as the spring came on, but in May, 1792, she had a second and more severe attack. Through 1793 her infirmities increased; she was unable to work or read, and sat silent, looking at the fire. During this time Cowper was her tender and self-sacrificing nurse, giving up his literary work to attend upon her. She died at East Dereham, in Norfolk, December 17, 1796, at the age of seventy-two, and was buried in St. Edmund's Chapel, in the East Dereham Church. The commentators vie with one another in praise of this poem. "No language on earth," remarks Hayley, "can exhibit a specimen of verse more exquisitely tender." "The calm of passionate despair," writes Canon Benham, "seems to reign over

these exquisite verses." "For fully fifty years," says Mr.
Oswald Crawfurd, "before the inditing of Cowper's poem to his
friend Mrs. Unwin, nothing that I can think of so simple, so
adequate, so inartificial, so full of suppressed pathos and tenderness had been written by any English poet as these exquisite
verses."

NOTES.

1. **The twentieth year**, etc. It was twenty years before the
date of this poem, viz., in 1773, that Cowper's third derangement
occurred, a derangement which was much more lasting in its
effects than the two previous ones, and which prevented his
projected marriage with Mrs. Unwin.

3. **the last**, *i.e.* the last year with our sky overcast ; the end
of the melancholia that overshadows both our lives.

5. **Thy spirits**, etc. Cowper's letters of this period frequently
refer to Mrs. Unwin's dejection of spirits as a consequence of her
illness. Lady Hesketh, in a letter to her sister Theodora, after
her visit to Olney in June, 1786, represents Mrs. Unwin as
"very far from grave ; on the contrary, she is cheerful and gay
and laughs *de bon cœur* upon the smallest provocation." And
again : "She seems to have by nature a great fund of gaiety."

7. **'Twas my distress.** Cowper attributed Mrs. Unwin's
breakdown in a great measure to her care and anxiety on his
account in his attacks of melancholia. Cf. *To Newton*, Oct. 2,
1787 : "Mrs. Unwin, whose poor bark is still held together,
though shattered by being tossed and agitated so long by the
side of mine," etc.

9. **needles**, knitting-needles. In the letter just quoted, Lady
Hesketh writes : "Her (Mrs. Unwin's) constant employment is
knitting stockings.... Our cousin (*i.e.* Cowper) has not for many
years worn any other than those of her manufacture. She knits
silk, cotton, and worsted. She sits knitting on one side of the
table, in her spectacles, and he on the other, reading to her
(when he is not employed in writing) in his." After her seizure
she entirely lost the use of her right hand and arm. Cf. also
Cowper's letter to Lady Hesketh, Dec. 6, 1785 : "Mrs. Unwin ...
sits knitting stockings at my elbow, with a degree of industry
worthy of Penelope herself. You will not think this an exagge-
ration when I tell you that I have not bought a pair these
twenty years, either of thread, silk, or worsted. In a letter to
Newton, April 25, 1793, Cowper says : "While I write, my
poor invalid, who is still unable to amuse herself either with book
or needle, sits silent at my side."

15. **Thy sight ... will.** Cf. *To Lady Hesketh*, Sept. 9,
1792, of Mrs. Unwin : "Her sight and her hand still fail her, so

that she can neither read nor work; mortifying circumstances both to her, who is never willingly idle." *Seconds* = supports, backs up.

18. all thy threads, etc. Your thread, as you knitted, had a kind of magical power, and has made my heart your prisoner; *i.e.* your kind care for my comfort has won my grateful love. Cf. the old English love-song: "My heart is fast and cannot *disentangle.*"

21. Thy indistinct impressions. The paralysis affected Mrs. Unwin's power of speech, so that she could with difficulty articulate at all. On May 24, 1792, Cowper writes to Lady Hesketh: "Her speech has been almost unintelligible from the moment that she was struck."

22. uttered in a dream. Cf. Tennyson, *A Dream of Fair Women,* 109, 110: "My voice was thick with sighs As in a dream."

26. Are still, *i.e.* continue to be.

31. The sun ... for me, life would have no happiness for me deprived of you. Cf. *To Newton,* June 24, 1791: "I love not the world, I trust, so much as to wish a place in it, when all my beloved shall have left it."

34. Thy hands, etc. See note to l. 15 above. **Force,** strength.

37. provest, dost experience.

39. Upheld by two. Cf. *To Newton,* June 12, 1793: "She (Mrs. Unwin) uses the orchard-walk daily, but always supported between two." And *To John Johnson,* September 6, 1793: "We walked after dinner in the orchard, Mrs. Unwin between Sam and me." Sam Roberts was the poet's faithful factotum, whom he had brought with him from the St. Albans Asylum.

42. no chill, no coldness or loss of affection.

THE CASTAWAY.

INTRODUCTION.

This poem was written on March 20, 1799, and first published in 1803. It is founded upon an incident related in Anson's Voyages, which the poet had heard read some months before. "It is," writes Southey, "the last original piece that he composed, and, all circumstances considered, one of the most affecting that ever was composed." Cowper sees a melancholy image of his own destiny in the fate of the poor sailor, who, washed overboard in a storm, struggled bravely with the waves, till at length, subdued by toil, he sank. The poet was at this time in a frame of mind to draw such parallels (see ll. 59, 60 below) : thus, writing from Mundesley to Lady Hesketh, August 27, 1795, he says: "At two miles distance on the coast is a solitary pillar of rock, that the crumbling cliff has left at the high-water mark. I have visited it twice, and have found it an emblem of myself. Torn from my natural connexions, I stand alone and expect the storm that shall displace me."

In reference to the title of this poem, it may be noted that at the time of the poet's third derangement, in 1773, we find him making use of these words : "My sin and my judgment are alike peculiar. *I am a castaway,* deserted and condemned" (see Bible, 1 *Cor.* ix. 27).

NOTES.

1. **involved,** in its Latin meaning of ' wrapt, enveloped.' Cf. note, p. 103, l. 49.

3. **such a destined wretch as I,** one, like myself, doomed to destruction. Cf. note, p. 112, ll. 88-107.

4. **headlong** is formed from *head* by the old adverbial suffix *-ling* or *-long* ; cf. *darkling, sidelong.*

7. **Albion.** See note, p. 112, l. 88.

8. **he.** Lord George Anson, born in 1697, being appointed commander of an expedition against the Spanish settlements in the Pacific Ocean, sailed in 1740 with five men-of-war, doubled Cape Horn in March, 1741, and reached Juan Fernandez. Leaving this place in September, he captured some prizes, burnt Paita, till in May, 1742, having only his ship the *Centurion* left, he crossed the southern ocean for China. After taking another prize, he sailed for England, which he reached June 15, 1744. In 1747 he commanded the Channel Fleet, and captured six French men-of-war. He died in 1762.

11. **He loved them both,** *i.e.* the sailor loved both Anson and Albion.

14. **Expert to swim,** for 'expert at swimming.'

17. **lasting,** persistent, prolonged.

18. **Supported,** etc. So Milton's Satan (*Par. Lost,* i. 191) bids consult—

> " What reinforcement we may gain from hope,
> If not, *what resolution from despair.*"

19. **nor his friends had failed,** *i.e.* nor would his friends have failed.

22. **pitiless perforce,** *i.e.* they were compelled by the blast to be or seem to be pitiless ; cf. l. 31 below.

27. the coop. The wooden hen-coops on deck are handy things to throw overboard to a drowning man.

the floated cord, a rope with a buoy attached to it.

33. flight. He knew that their only means of safety lay in driving before the storm; it was impossible to bring the ship about.

37. He is strictly a demonstrative (= that man), not a personal pronoun here.

40. His destiny repelled, resisted his doom.

43. his transient respite past. His death was delayed for a short time by his exertions;—an absolute clause.

49. wept him, wrote an elegy to lament his loss: as Milton did when his friend King (Lycidas) was drowned.

the page. "A Voyage round the World, 1740-44, compiled from Lord Anson's papers and official documents," by "Richard Walter, M.A.," was published in 1748.

52. Is wet, etc. The narrative shows that Anson was full of pity for the poor seaman's fate.

53. tears by bards, etc. Whether the dead are mourned by poets in their verses, or (as in the present instance) by heroes (such as Anson) in the narrative of their exploits—in either case, their memory will live.

55-60. I therefore, etc. Hence (since this man's sad fate is already immortalized) my object in telling his story is not to perpetuate his memory, but I tell it because the unhappy are fond of finding in the misfortune of others a parallel to their own. See Introduction.

59. still, ever, continually.

61. No voice divine, etc. Alluding to the incident related in the Bible, *Matt.* viii. 23-26, when Christ "rebuked the winds and the sea; and there was a great calm."

62. No light propitious, no kindly light, such as, in the sailor's case, that of the moon; cf. l. 1 above.

64. we perished. The sudden change of subject (from "he" to "we") here has a powerful, almost startling, effect.

STRADA'S NIGHTINGALE.

INTRODUCTION.

This translation from the Latin of Vincent Bourne (see Introduction to *The Jackdaw*, p. 74) was first published in 1803. Bourne's poem is based upon a celebrated picture by John Strada, an eminent artist and animal-painter, born at Bruges in 1536, who went early to Italy and settled at Florence, where he executed many fine works.

NOTES.

1. **touched his reed**, played upon his reed-pipe ; he touched the stops with his fingers.

Philomel *Philomela* is the Greek word for 'nightingale,' because, according |to the legend, Philomela, the daughter of Pandion, king of Athens, was changed into this bird.

4. **numbers.** See note, p. 112, l. 71.

9. **dared**, dared to attempt, ventured upon.

rising as he rose, raising her voice in correspondence with his "loftier tones."

14. **songstress.** See note, p. 71, l. 23.

THE COLUBRIAD.

INTRODUCTION.

This poem was first published in 1803. It was probably written in the autumn of 1782, since Cowper relates the incident in a letter to Unwin dated August 3 of that year: "Passing from the greenhouse to the barn, I saw three kittens (for we have so many in our retinue) looking with fixed attention at something which lay on the threshold of the door, coiled up. I took but little notice of them at first ; but a loud hiss engaged me to attend more closely, when behold—a viper ! the largest I remember to have seen, rearing itself, darting its forked tongue, and ejaculating the aforementioned hiss at the nose of a kitten almost in contact with his lips. I ran into the hall for a hoe with a long handle, with which I intended to assail him, and returning in a few seconds missed him : he was gone and I feared had escaped me. Still however the kitten sat watching immoveably upon the same spot. I concluded, therefore, that sliding between the door and the threshold, he had found his way out of the garden into the yard. I went round immediately, and there found him in close conversation with the old cat, whose curiosity, being excited by so novel an appearance, inclined her to pat his head repeatedly with her fore foot ; with her claws however sheathed, and not in anger, but in the way of philosophical (*i.e.* scientific) inquiry and examination. To prevent her falling a victim to so laudable an exercise of her talents, I interposed in a moment with the hoe, and performed upon him an act of decapitation, which though not immediately mortal proved so in the end.

Colubriad is formed from Lat. *coluber*, gen. *colubri*, a snake, on the model of "Iliad," "Dunciad," etc., and so means a poem with a snake for its hero or subject.

NOTES.

1. **a door nailed fast**, the barn-door; see Introduction. This old barn was situated between the yard (l. 29) at the back of Orchard Side, Cowper's house at Olney, and the long, narrow garden which lay behind the yard, and in which was the green-house.

11. **viper.** From Lat. *vipera*, short for *vivipara*, producing live young.

Count de Grasse's queue. The French admiral, Count de Grasse, was a well-known figure at this time, since in January of this year (1782) he had been defeated by Hood off St. Christopher's in the West Indies, and the following April had been defeated and captured with his ship, the *Ville de Paris*, of 100 guns, by Rodney. He wore his periwig with the queue, or pigtail, very long, and with the end turned up and tied into a loop with a riband—a peculiarity which formed a prominent object in the caricatures of the day, and so would be familiar to Cowper and his contemporaries. Gillray has a caricature entitled "Rodney introducing De Grasse."

12. **forkèd tongue.** The "double tongue" of a snake is of course quite harmless. It serves chiefly as a feeler.

13. **full.** An adverb, as is *close* in l. 25 below.

19. **Dutch hoe.** One of the fashion used in Holland.

27. **door-sill**, threshold; see Introduction.

29. **No doubt but I shall find him** = there is no doubt except that I shall find him; *i.e.* there is no doubt to prevent my finding him. We now generally say 'No doubt (that) I shall find him.'

33. **with velvet paw**, with "claws sheathed"; see Introduction.

34. **erst.** See note, p. 132, l. 100.

41. **never ... no more.** The double negative, a vulgarism in modern English, is introduced by way of playful emphasis. Cf. note, p. 89, l. 16.

ON A MISCHIEVOUS BULL.

INTRODUCTION.

This poem was first published in *Poems*, 1808. The owner of the bull was Cowper's neighbour, Mr. Throckmorton. It is

not improbably this bull that is mentioned in a passage in which
Dean Burgon describes the poet's narrative powers : "His eye
would suddenly kindle, and all his face become lighted up
with the fun of the story, before he opened his lips to speak.
At last he began to relate some ludicrous incident. ... A bull
had frightened him, and caused him to clear a hedge with undue
precipitancy.   His 'shorts' became seriously lacerated ; and
the consternation with which their modest occupant effected
his retreat home—holding his garments together in order that
his calamity might escape detection—was made extravagantly
diverting."

NOTES.

2. **this place.** Weston Park, belonging to Mr. Throckmorton.

14. **secure** has here perhaps its older meaning of 'free from
care or anxiety,' rather than its commoner meaning of 'safe.'
Cf. *The Jackdaw*, 15, and note.

22. **So I,** 'provided that I ; so long as I.' The full construction
is 'if it be so that I,' and *so* seems to mean 'in this way, on
these terms' (see Abbott, *Shaks. Gr.*, § 133).

23. **The angry Muse**, etc., *i.e.* I write this indignant poem on
your expulsion. See note, p. 98, l. 51.

24. **claps,** abruptly closes, bangs to.

INDEX TO NOTES.

[The references are to the pages. *Italics* denote subjects.]

142

Breath, 72.
Brennus, 79.
Bright-studded, 126.
Britannia, 128.
Browne, 69.
Buffet, 127.
Burning word, 78.
Buskin, 122.
Byron, 92.

C

Caesar, 110.
Caledonia, 126.
Calender, 89.
Cambrian, 104.
Campion, 70.
Cap, 125.
Carries weight, 91.
Cassiopeïa, 126.
Catullus, 96.
Charged, 117, 126.
Chattel, 127.
Chaucer, 90, 92, 115.
Cheapside, 90.
Cheat, 86.
Cherup, 107.
Chevy Chase, 93.
Church, 75.
Church-going bell, 67.
Clough, A. H., 112.
Cognate object, 75, 91 110, 131.
Coleridge, 89.
Colman, 86, 121, 122.
Colonnade, 94.
Conditional Imperative, 75, 104.
Conditional without 'if,' 66, 69, 71, 75, 110.
Confectionary, 111.
Connoisseur, The, 122.
Conventional epithets, 131.
Count de Grasse, 140.
Crash, 103.
Crop, 71.
Cumulation, 71, 115.
Cup, 117.
Curious, 77.
Cynthio, 74.

D

Dapple, 104.
Dear (noun), 89.
Debonair, 130.
Denham, 64.
Dense and rare, 99.
Dickens, 89.
Diodorus Siculus, 81.
Donne, Roger, 87.
Dormitory, 75.
Double negative, 140.
Dray, 63.
Drayton, 63.
Dream, 94, 107, 122, 136.
Druids, 78.
Dryden, 82, 110.
Dunstan, 92.
Dupe of to-morrow, 110.

E

Eagles (Roman), 79.
Ebon, 97.
Eke, 89.
Ellipse, 66, 131.
Elysian, 110.
'Em, 76.
Erst, 132, 140.
Etna, 81.
Exhale, 120.

F

Fair (noun), 63, 70, 124.
Fandango, 101.
Fast, 83, 98, 117.
Fieldfare, 102.
Fire, 80.
Flag, 106.
Flageolet, } 96.
Flute, }
Flight reversed, 112, 113.
Flora, 69.
Fop, 133.
For that, 89.
For why, 92.
Forkèd tongue, 140.
Fox (C. J.), 120.
Fraught, 74.

GLASGOW : PRINTED AT THE UNIVERSITY PRESS BY ROBERT MACLEHOSE AND CO.

www.ingramcontent.com/pod-product-compliance
Lightning Source LLC
Chambersburg PA
CBHW030846270326
41928CB00007B/1235